HOCUS POCUS

IN FOCUS

THE THINKING FAN'S GUIDE TO DISNEY'S HALLOWEEN CLASSIC

Books by Aaron Wallace

The Thinking Fan's Guide to Walt Disney World: Magic Kingdom
The Thinking Fan's Guide to Walt Disney World: Epcot
Hocus Pocus in Focus: The Thinking Fan's Guide to Disney's Halloween Classic

Praise for *The Thinking Fan's Guide to Walt Disney World*

"Intelligent, with a hint of the humorous mixed in for good measure." — Heidi Strawser, *Heidi's Head*

"Insanely readable." — Andrew Tipton, *Disney Hipsters*

"It's fun to know someone took a deeper look." — Rudy Maxa, Emmy Winner and host of the most widely syndicated travel radio program in the world

"Few could come to the same brilliant conclusions." — Alex Reif, *LaughingPlace*.com

"Descriptive, contemplative... so comprehensive... as recommended for erudite armchair travelers as it is for starry-eyed tourists!" — James Cox, Editor-In-Chief, *The Midwest Book Review*

"A must-have for WDW fans!" — Jeff DePaoli, *Dizney Coast to Coast*

"I was curious going in to see what is considered a Thinking Fan's guide... and as luck would have it, they think like us geeks think!" — Jason Dziegielewski, *DisneyGeek*.com

"It's like giving every Disney guest... their own Disney historian as a guide." — Natalie Reiner, *Ink and Paint Blog*

HOCUS POCUS

IN FOCUS

THE THINKING FAN'S GUIDE
TO DISNEY'S HALLOWEEN CLASSIC

AARON WALLACE

Foreword by Thora Birch

Published by Pensive Pen Publishing, Orlando, Florida
www.pensivepenpublishing.com

First Edition
Printed in the United States
Cover design by Rob Yeo
Foreword by Thora Birch
Afterword by Mick Garris
Edited by Sally E. Bahner
ISBN: 978-0-9980592-0-4
Library of Congress Control Number: 2016953352

About the Author

Aaron Wallace first started thinking critically about The Walt Disney Company's artistic output during his time at The University of North Carolina at Chapel Hill, where he earned a Bachelor of Arts degree in both Communication Studies (with a concentration in Media Studies) and English. While there, he taught a recitation course in analyzing children's literature, with an emphasis on Disney's adaptations in theme parks and film.

Today, Aaron is a writer and attorney, having earned a Juris Doctor degree from Wake Forest University. He is also a professional entertainment critic, having published more than two hundred movie, television, and music reviews to an audience of millions. Since 2004, he's been a part of the writing staff at DVDizzy.com, one of the internet's most accessed sites for entertainment journalism.

In addition to writing, Aaron hosts *Zip-A-Dee-Doo-Pod*, the web's longest-running podcast dedicated to all things Disney. Apple has recognized the show as one of its "Featured Travel Podcasts," and *Zip-A-Dee-Doo-Pod* can often be found among the top-ranking downloads on the iTunes Travel charts. Aaron also appears as a regular co-host on *The Hub Podcast*, another popular show devoted to having fun with Disney.

Aaron lives in Orlando, Florida, where he visits the Walt Disney World Resort on at least a weekly basis and shares his adventures on Twitter, using the handle @aaronspod.

His website is available at www.AaronWallaceOnline.com.

Dedication

Dedicated to:

Luke Bonanno, who gave me my first opportunity to write about movies professionally.

In tribute to:

Garry Marshall, who passed away during the writing of this book and whose impact on *Hocus Pocus* is indelible.

Table of Contents

Foreword

By Thora Birch

When I was ten years old, I undoubtedly shared similarities with the character of Dani in *Hocus Pocus*. I was a dedicated Halloween aficionado and known for a kind of precociousness, as was she, among other parallels.

So many great memories remain from my time spent on the film... the smell of the Sanderson sisters' cottage — I never DID get to climb that water wheel, but OH how I wanted to — and struggling constantly to keep that hat on my head.

I will never forget the fun I had tearing up the set (gorgeously and luxuriously crafted by William Sandell and Nancy Patton) with the wonderful and lovely Vinessa Shaw and Omri Katz.

How could I forget Kenny Ortega's energy, or Kathy Najimy's laugh, or being suspended in the air with Bette Midler in an uncomfortable harness and her singing "Wind Beneath My Wings" to comfort me between takes? I've said it before, and I don't mind repeating it: I don't think I've ever had more *fun* on a set than I did while filming *Hocus Pocus*.

Filmmaking itself has evolved so much since the era in which the film was made. In 1992, when *Hocus Pocus* began production, a film of its size and scope took about three-and-a-half months to shoot. And the budget, at $28 million, was considered even then not to be too pricy — generous for a 'family' movie, yes, but by no means bloated, considering it carried with it the machinery of Disney and the force of The Divine Miss M.

When you work on a film for three months, a different kind of relationship is established with the cast and crew than when you're on a film for, say, three weeks to a month. Bonds grow a little stronger, the experience lingers with you a little longer (a LOT longer in this case), and in many ways, I miss those days when waiting three hours for lighting in between shots — not scenes, mind you — was absolutely the norm. I'm thankful *Hocus Pocus* was made when it was. It is very difficult to imagine the film working as it does had it been made in any other era.

For me, the movie was an introduction to the technological advances the film industry would witness and champion in the following decades. Witches were flying well before Neo's kicks… and I'll never forget getting a preview of the process that turned our black cats into the soothing and innocent personality of Binx (which was new CGI tech that had not been used much at the time).

While making the movie, I was simply having fun on and off the set, loving every second of Salem, Massachusetts; the Disney lot; Warner's famed backlot; and being constantly surrounded by items representing my favorite holiday for months.

I didn't know the film would turn out simultaneously eerie AND flamboyant (as it hit my eyes when released). I didn't know anyone would ever analyze the Spielbergian 'pixie dust' elements of the film or its placement amidst holiday classics in general. I wasn't aware of the film's feminist overtones. I didn't consider the cultural ramifications of the witches targeting 'virgins,' and I certainly would never have even considered the potential classification of *Hocus Pocus* as a horror film — all things explored in this book.

I was merely excited to be part of a Disney movie that seemed a little darker and a Halloween film that was kind of a comedy. I was thrilled to be working with Bette Midler, Kathy Najimy, Sarah Jessica Parker, and our esteemed director, Kenny Ortega, very much a "big kid" himself, in my opinion.

I'll admit that when the reviews came out and opening weekend was a disappointment at best, I was very hurt and confused. I couldn't understand how critics didn't appreciate the dedication and passion Ortega, Midler, and the cast and crew had thrown into the film. I had thought it was for SURE going to be a hit (*I* loved the movie...), and I was pretty surprised it didn't have an instant and permanent cultural impact, resulting in people dressing up as Winifred, Mary, and Sarah on Halloween.

So, I sucked it up and moved on to more mature roles, exploring adolescence in the early '70s with *Now and Then*... suburban malaise with films like *American Beauty* and *Ghost World*... I even played around with the genre of actual horror in films like *Train* and *Dark Corners*, and I rarely thought of *Hocus Pocus* much, other than to sometimes watch it around Halloween.

My relationship with the film largely disappeared until one day I woke up and realized something unique and surprising had happened... audiences rediscovered the film and decided to talk about it online. A LOT. Somewhere along the line, older siblings started watching it with baby bro and sis, young parents played it for their trick-or-treat-obsessed toddlers, and now the Disney Channel really, REALLY, likes rerunning it (pretty much year-round but specifically September through October).

On a more personal note, the most surprising thing about *Hocus Pocus* is that out of all the other roles I've played that have gotten a fair amount of attention for one reason or the other — to this day — if people recognize me and decide to say something about my work... they usually wind up asking me to appease their suspicion that I am "the little girl from *Hocus Pocus*."

Because of all of that, and the amount of work and, yes, *thought* that went into this book, I was so happy Aaron Wallace reached out to me to write the foreword. Because I, like you (hopefully), am at the end of the day... just another fan of this delightful movie. And I hope you enjoy reading this book (and re-watching the film) at least *half* as much as I enjoyed being a part of it.

About Thora Birch

Named after the Norse god of thunder, Thora was born and raised in Los Angeles, CA. At the age of four, a close family friend noticed her outgoing personality and uncanny knack for imitating commercials. At the age of six (and 40 national commercials later), she landed a spot on the NBC sitcom, "Day by Day" (1988) and won a Young Artist Award for her introductory performance in the family film, *Purple People Eater* (1988) with Shelley Winters and Neil Patrick Harris. Shortly thereafter, she landed another role in a short-lived sitcom, "Parenthood" (1990), based on the film of the same name and co-starring Leonardo DiCaprio.

By the age of nine, Thora had her life pretty much figured out; she told the *L.A. Times* that she planned on becoming a director by the age of 24, then spending a year ice skating, another year as a police officer, and finally becoming a singer. She picked up her last name (having previously been credited simply as "Thora") and gained widespread praise for her turn in *Paradise* (1991) as a neighborhood tomboy living next door to Melanie Griffith and Don Johnson. She scored a high-profile supporting role as Harrison Ford's daughter in *Patriot Games* (1992) and reprised the role in *Clear and Present Danger* (1994). In between those two films, she kept busy with *All I Want for Christmas* (1992), *Hocus Pocus* (1993), and *Monkey Trouble* (1994). In '95, Birch graduated to adolescent territory with her turn in Demi Moore's first producing effort, *Now and Then* (1995), and she followed that up with the top-billed role in the snowy adventure, *Alaska* (1996).

She started out 1999 with the made-for-TV *Night Ride Home* and ended it with the Academy Awards' 1999 pick for Best Picture, *American Beauty*. Reaching this higher level of success launched a series of edgier and more mature roles for Thora in *The Smokers* (2000), *Dungeons & Dragons* (2000), *Ghost World* (2001, for which she received a Best Actress Golden Globe nomination), *The Hole* (2002), *Homeless to Harvard* (2003, Emmy nomination), and The Weinstein Company's *Slingshot* (2005), followed by a dual role in *Dark Corners* (2006). She has been seen in *Train*, *Deadline*, and *Pregnancy Pact*. Her first producing effort, *Petunia*, is available on iTunes and Netflix.

After taking a break to focus on school, Thora resumed her acting career in 2016 to great fanfare. She appeared in Carlton Cuse and Ryan Condal's hit television series, "Colony."

In the film world, Thora next stars opposite Brian Cox, JJ Feild, and Rosanna Arquette in the independent feature, *The Etruscan Smile*; in the political thriller *Public Affairs;* and plays Emilia Clarke's sister opposite Jack Huston and Johnny Knoxville in the drama *Above Suspicion*, with all three scheduled for release in 2017.

Introduction

Hocus Pocus has been part of my life for *most* of my life, and I suspect that's true for many of you too. I don't remember much of Halloween before it, and I can't imagine Halloween without it. For a quarter-century now, the movie has been a gem for my generation. These days, it's familiar to just about anyone of *any* age, even to those who still haven't seen it.

And yet there is a notion out there that *Hocus Pocus* isn't worth its circle of salt. "Harmlessly hokey," the critics of 1993 called it, "mediocre" and "muddled."[1] In 2015, Vox.com featured an op/ed entitled *Hocus Pocus Is a Garbage Movie That Doesn't Deserve Your Nostalgia.*[2]

Garbage? Sisters, did you *hear* what he called you?

Well, you know what they say — one fan's trash is another fan's book material. At its core, *The Thinking Fan's Guide* book series is about thinking outside the box while still having fun with the things we love. I love movies, especially Disney movies, and it's gratifying to know that so many others love them like I do too.

But we don't fall in love with movies for no reason, and we don't even need to assume they're mere "guilty pleasures" because critics of several decades ago wrote them off. *Hocus Pocus* certainly isn't the first film to eventually find a large and passionate audience in spite of critical rejection. And truth be told, some of those earned their scorn. I suspect, however, people are responding to something special in *Hocus Pocus*, and this book aims to explore that with a sense of whimsy, wonder, and creative liberty.

There are twelve chapters here, and eleven of those will watch *Hocus Pocus* from a different angle. Another, toward the end of the book, will look at the movie's presence in theme parks instead. The book also closes with an epilogue looking toward a potential *Hocus Pocus* sequel, as well as trivia-filled fun facts and movie recommendations for fans.

Walt Disney reportedly said, "We just make the pictures and let the professors tell us what they mean." Well, I'm not your professor, and this isn't a textbook, but it's in that same spirit that I hope to put our collective fingers on what *Hocus Pocus* "means," even if sometimes the meaning wasn't apparent to the filmmakers themselves at the time of production. Even authors sometimes only realize what they've made in retrospect.

A central tenet of this book is that *Hocus Pocus* is a fine and worthy film, and it ought to be enjoyed just as richly as any other, even as we acknowledge that none of us — myself included — could ever read an actor or filmmaker's mind. Still, we bring a lot to a movie as members of its audience, and I think the real fun of loving movies is what goes on in our own minds and spirits while we watch.

To be sure, *Hocus Pocus* has its imperfections. So does *Citizen Kane*. Film appreciation isn't so much about counting anachronisms as surveying the whole of a movie and asking what works (or doesn't) and, more importantly, how and why it works.

So while I certainly don't contend this witchy 1993 comedy ought to appear alongside Orson Welles's masterpiece in AFI's next list of the 100 greatest movies of all time, I do think it lends itself to thoughtful appreciation.

In writing this book, I assume my readers will have seen the movie at least once before, so consider this sentence an all-purpose spoiler warning. Still, it might be helpful to briefly bring ourselves back up to speed on the story (and to just quickly brush up on our "Hollywood 101" too).

Haven't Seen the Movie in a While?

That's okay. Ideally, you will read this book after having recently revisited the film. With annual TV airings and reasonably priced Blu-ray and DVD releases (the former has an excellent HD transfer), that's easier than ever. And I hope, after finishing the book, you'll feel inspired to watch the movie again and discover whole new worlds within it. But this book isn't written exclusively for *Hocus Pocus* "super fans." Casual familiarity, coupled with the plot synopsis on the next page, should suffice.

The Disney Story in Four Paragraphs

Walter Elias Disney was born in Chicago on December 5, 1901 and moved to the small town of Marceline, Missouri with his family when he was four. The Disneys faced financial struggles throughout Walt's childhood, much of which was spent moving around the country in search of work. By the time he was 18, Walt had started a career as a cartoonist, finding a few small successes over the next ten years. In 1928, his life changed forever with the theatrical release of *Steamboat Willie*, introducing the world to Mickey Mouse. Mickey was a hit and paved the way for the first-ever animated feature film, *Snow White and the Seven Dwarfs*. Widely expected to fail, *Snow White* surprised everyone in 1937 by becoming one of the biggest box office achievements of all time, a distinction it retains to this day.

Walt made many more movies after *Snow White*, but few of them saw real success until the 1950s, when audiences in America and around the world started clamoring for almost everything the Disney Studios produced. In addition to a string of popular movies, Walt also hit it big on television, a market most film producers didn't want to touch. "The Mickey Mouse Club" and serials like "Davy Crockett" took the country by storm. It was also during the 1950s that Walt opened California's Disneyland, the world's first true theme park.

Walt died in December 1966, but his company continued on, eventually opening Walt Disney World in Florida and its first two theme parks, Magic Kingdom and EPCOT Center. But without Walt, the Disney brand struggled to find its identity during the 1970s and early '80s. That changed when Walt's nephew, Roy E. Disney, recruited then-Paramount CEO Michael Eisner to take the reigns in 1984, triggering what many have come to call "The Disney Renaissance." From animation to live-action, theme parks, corporate acquisitions, and beyond, business was booming at Disney again.

The 1990s were especially successful, and the films from that period generally enjoyed a walloping response from family audiences of all ages. *The Little Mermaid* (1989), *Beauty and the Beast* (1991), *Aladdin* (1992), and *The Lion King* (1994) were instrumental in defining "The Disney Decade." At the same time, Disney was enjoying success with grown-up audiences under its Touchstone Pictures label, created as a means for distributing less family-friendly films. *Hocus Pocus* came to theaters under the Walt Disney Pictures label in the summer of 1993.

The *Hocus Pocus* Story in Four Paragraphs

Salem, Massachusetts, October, 1993 — In a flashback, **Mrs. Olin** (Kathleen Freeman) teaches her high school class about a local legend of great renown: the tale of the three Sanderson sisters. On All Hallows' Eve 1693, a teenaged boy named **Thackery Binx** (Sean Murray) awoke to find his little sister, **Emily** (Amanda Shepherd), lured to the woods by a witch's spell. As night fell, Thackery snuck into the witches' cottage and found the three Sandersons, **Winifred** ("Winnie," Bette Midler), **Mary** (Kathy Najimi), and **Sarah** (Sarah Jessica Parker) sucking the life force out of his young sister, and it made them younger and more beautiful right away. They caught Thackery and turned him into a black cat (voiced by Jason Marsden), cursing him to a life of feline immortality. Soon after, the townsfolk arrived, seized the witches, and hanged them. But just before they died, Winifred's spell book — stitched from human flesh and possessing an actual eye — presented her with a curse: on a future Halloween night, when the moon is full, a virgin would light a black-flame candle and summon the witches back from the dead.

Max Dennison (Omri Katz) isn't impressed with Mrs. Olin's story, even though his classmates eat it up. He and his sister **Dani** (Thora Birch) are new to Salem, having just moved from Los Angeles, and Max misses home. He does fancy a beautiful young classmate named **Allison** (Vinessa Shaw), but she doesn't seem interested. As if that weren't bad enough, Max has to deal with two bullies, **Jay** (Tobias Jelinek) and **Ernie** (also known as "**Ice**," played by Larry Bagby), who always seem to show up at the worst possible times.

Max reluctantly agrees to take Dani trick-or-treating, but his spirits lift when they knock on Allison's door. The three of them decide to sneak into the old Sanderson cottage. There, Max — a virgin — shows off by lighting the infamous black-flame candle, even as Thackery (still alive as a cat) tries to stop him. The lights go out, green mist glows from beneath the floor, and the Sanderson sisters are back faster than you can say "Terminator." The kids escape, but the witches quickly put plans in motion to suck the lives out of the children of Salem. Their spell only brought them back for one night, you see, and unless they're able to ingest enough life force to achieve immortality, they'll perish at daybreak. The only problem? They can't remember the life force potion, and Max stole Winifred's spell book on his way out the door.

The witches chase after the book but fall into a trap and are burned alive. Dani and the gang celebrate, but little do they know that the black-flame candle's magic won't permit the witches an early demise. They return, break into the Dennison house, and steal the spell book and Dani too. Sarah casts a spell on all the children of Salem, luring them to the cottage, where a soul-sucking potion awaits them. But Max and Allison destroy the potion, rescue Dani, and take cover in the local graveyard (because witches can't step foot on holy ground). The Sandersons follow them there and do battle from the sky. Max attempts to sacrifice himself for his sister, downing the last surviving drop of potion, but it doesn't work. The witches aren't able to consume his life force, and sunrise arrives, vanquishing them. Thackery's spirit is released at long last.

Background Information

Hocus Pocus arrived in U.S. theaters on July 16, 1993, directed by Kenny Ortega and rated PG by the Motion Picture Association of America (MPAA). The screenplay is by Neil Cuthbert and Mick Garris, with a story by Garris and producer David Kirschner. Steven Haft and Bonnie Bruckheimer co-produce. Meanwhile, Ralph Winter executive produces and Garris co-executive produces. Hiro Narita serves as cinematographer, Peter E. Berger as editor, William Sandell as production designer,

Nancy Patton as art director, Rosemary Brandenburg as set decorator, and Mary Vogt as costumer designer. John Debney and James Horner provide the film score, with lyrics by Brock Walsh. "I Put a Spell on You," originally written by Screamin' Jay Hawkins, is produced and arranged by Marc Shaiman and performed by Bette Midler. Joseph Malone performs "Witchcraft" by Cy Coleman and Carolyn Leigh. Tobias Jelinek and Larry Bagby perform "Row, Row, Row Your Boat."

The film runs 96 minutes and is available on DVD, Blu-ray, and through digital download from Walt Disney Studios Home Entertainment. The soundtrack is available from Intrada Records, in partnership with Walt Disney Records. The film is occasionally presented in select Cinemark theaters as part of the officially licensed DisneyScreen program.

An Unofficial Companion

This book is not affiliated with The Walt Disney Company (or any of its affiliates or subsidiaries), and it has not been submitted for their approval or review. The thoughts and opinions expressed in the pages and chapters ahead are solely my own, except where otherwise credited, and do not necessarily reflect the views or opinions of The Walt Disney Company, Walt Disney Pictures, Walt Disney Parks and Resorts, Walt Disney Imagineering, or the cast or crew of *Hocus Pocus*.

Cast

Bette Midler	Winifred Sanderson
Sarah Jessica Parker	Sarah Sanderson
Kathy Najimy	Mary Sanderson
Omri Katz	Max Dennison
Thora Birch	Dani Dennison
Vinessa Shaw	Allison
Amanda Shepherd	Emily Binx
Larry Bagby III	Ernie, a.k.a. "Ice"
Tobias Jelinek	Jay

Stephanie Faracy	Jenny Dennison
Charles Rocket	Dave Dennison
Doug Jones	Billy Butcherson
Karyn Malchus	Headless Billy Butcherson
Sean Murray	Thackery Binx (in human form)
Steve Voboril	Elijah
Norbert Weisser	Thackery's Father
Kathleen Freeman	Mrs. Olin
Don Yesso	Bus Driver
Michael McGrady	Cop
Leigh Hamilton	Cop's Girlfriend
Joseph Malone	Singer (skeleton band leader)
Jason Marsden	Thackery Binx (voice)
Garry Marshall	The Master
Penny Marshall	The Master's Wife

A Brief Glossary

Throughout the book, I use several terms of art that apply to movies in general or to Disney works in particular. They will be familiar to some movie fans and maybe not to others, but a few definitions from the world of film studies could prove useful going forward. (Don't worry; you don't need to memorize them.)

agency. A character's ability to act independently and make decisions for herself or himself.

auteur. The French word for "author," *auteur* refers to a filmmaker whose personal influence or artistic control over a movie is so great the filmmaker is regarded as the movie's author.[3] "Auteur theory" refers to the conventional notion that a movie should be interpreted as a director's work, much like a novel is interpreted as the work of its author.

cinematography. The art of making creative choices involving lighting, camera motion, camera position, and frame composition (that is, what the camera does and does not "see") to achieve a given aesthetic result.

cue. In film scores (see below), a piece of music performed and recorded so it fits within the precise time requirements of a given shot (see below) or scene.

mise-en-scène. Roughly translated from French, it literally means "setting the stage" or "placing in the scene." In film studies, the term refers to everything we see within a given shot, as well as the way in which those things are lit, positioned, colored, costumed, etc. Critics consider this concept important because (generally speaking) nothing appears the way it does within the film frame by accident. In other words, movies are artificial constructs, and everything within the frame might be considered the result of a choice. The entire *mise-en-scène* contributes to our understanding of a given shot or scene.

narrative. Though it is a word with many important meanings, for our purposes here, "narrative" is best understood as the way in which a story is presented. Whereas "plot" refers to what happens in a story, "narrative" refers to the way in which that story is told: the sequencing of events, the use of flashback, the rhythm and pace of the storytelling, where the story begins and ends, etc. When filmmakers construct a narrative, they make many decisions about how to tell their story (and, just as importantly, how not to tell it).

oeuvre. The collective works of a director, artist, author, or composer.

score. Music composed to accompany a film. Sometimes colloquially referred to as "background music" or the "soundtrack," though those terms each have slightly different meanings. Film scores are primarily instrumental; however, they occasionally feature vocal performances, especially by choirs.

shot. An image uninterrupted by transitions or cuts. A shot begins when we cut to a new image and ends when we cut from it. A scene may be made up of one shot or many. For example, in a scene with two characters talking, the camera may cut to a close-up of one person's face for 20 seconds, then to the other person for 30 seconds, then back to the first person for 40 seconds. In total, this would be a single scene, lasting 90 seconds, consisting of three shots.

subtext. Ideas, themes, messages, or meanings that are not explicitly or overtly addressed within a movie but which nevertheless become apparent when audiences consider symbols, connotations, allusions, and other such devices.[4]

text. Film scholars often refer to movies as "texts." The idea is that we can "read" a movie like we read a book. When we read books, we look "between the lines" and consider literary elements such as foreshadowing, mood, tone, implication, etc. We can find these same elements in movies.

trope. A situation or literary device that tends to recur in different works of literature or film (e.g. widely reused plot patterns, stock characters, motifs, figures of speech, archetypes, clichés, etc.).

A Note on Style

In this book, the titles of movies, short films, musical albums, tours, and books are italicized. The titles of poems, songs, television series, and episode titles appear in quotation marks. The titles of places and theme park attractions will be capitalized without italics or quotation marks. As is common practice, when referring to Walt Disney, the person, I will generally use "Walt." When referring to the Walt Disney Company or the executives and creatives representing the company collectively, I will generally use "Disney," except where context dictates otherwise.

A Word on Accuracy

Should anything in this book strike your curiosity, or if you happen to find anything you believe to be in error, please contact me directly with questions or suggestions at book@aaronwallaceonline.com. You can also contact me on Twitter via @aaronspod. I encourage you to visit my website, www.AaronWallaceOnline.com, and sign up to receive important updates.

A Little More Magic

Writing a *Hocus Pocus* "booOOOook" has been incredibly rewarding. I hope you come away with a newfound appreciation for the movie. If I've done my job, the next time you watch it, you'll find so much more than you ever realized was in *Hocus Pocus*. I suppose some might say a whole book about this of all movies is nothing but "just a bunch of hocus pocus" itself — or that taking the time to dig a little deeper is silly — but as Winifred says to her sisters while flipping through the pages of her own book, "We can do better than that, I think."

I sincerely hope you enjoy these thoughts and reflections. Perhaps you will even be inspired toward new ones of your own. Happy reading!

Aaron Wallace
Orlando, Florida

Chapter One

The *Home Alone* of Halloween

Something is happening. *Hocus Pocus*, that weird little Clark Bar of a movie my generation loved — and feared — but no one else ever cared for is emerging as more of a Reese's Peanut Butter Cup, celebrated by all.

Twenty years or so after its release, just in time for its original audience to grow up, gain employment, and rebuff "old media," *Hocus Pocus* transformed from forgotten fluff to bankable buzz. Now, September begins what online magpies call "*Hocus Pocus* season," when the web goes *HoPo* loco and social media manufactures Sanderson sister memes like candy kisses on a conveyor belt. Once a box office flop, the movie is now a bona fide phenomenon, juicy clickbait for Halloween-lovin' millennials and the adjacent generations they've lured into embracing this oddball comedy with a sinister side.

In 2015, *Entertainment Weekly* created a quiz inviting readers to compare themselves to their favorite "pop culture witch." The header pictured just three candidates: the Wicked Witch of the West, *Harry Potter*'s Hermione Granger, and Winifred Sanderson of *Hocus Pocus*.[1] That same year, Walt Disney World's Magic Kingdom announced a new addition to its Not-So-Scary Halloween Party: a *Hocus Pocus* stage show. The party dates sold out, the show earned rave reviews, and the event earned headlines everywhere from CBS and MTV to *Playbill* and *USA Today*.[2] Even still, nothing seems to squelch the public's demand for a sequel, the annual "will they or won't they?" having become a seasonal staple.[3]

Hocus Pocus has evolved into a film with real pop-culture currency, perhaps soon becoming one of the most watched movies of our time. Holidays are fertile ground for film classics. Most of us revisit the movies we *love* every year or two, and ones we only *like* far less frequently than that. But holiday pictures (as they were once called) are inherently annual beings. Even if we watch them only once every October 31 or December 25, that adds up to ten or twenty viewings across a couple of decades, and I'd hazard a guess there are only a handful of films you've seen that many times. Repetition is at the heart of festivity. Movies can become as integral to our celebrations as songs, scents, and foods. That's especially true of movies the whole family can watch, meaning children might easily score a dozen viewings or more before they're of age for coarser fare.

But whereas Christmas family films abound, relatively few in the Halloween realm had gone to theaters prior to *Hocus Pocus*.[4] So it was poised to become for the trick-or-treat season what *Home Alone* had become for Christmas three years prior: a modern holiday classic.

Bear in mind, though, *Home Alone* broke box office records while still in theaters. It wasn't until The Disney Channel and ABC Family rolled out endless re-airings some years later that *Hocus Pocus* began scoring impressive numbers. Now, it's nearly as reliable a channel-surfing find as *A Christmas Story* in late December. Meanwhile, Disney now counts the DVD among its top autumn sellers, outranking most other studios' *new-release* titles, fall after fall for more than a decade.[5] Like a black cat, the movie has another life to live, and this time around, people are paying attention.

The critics of 1993 were about as kind to *Hocus Pocus* as Justin Bieber has been to Bette Midler. ("This Britt Meddler," he told *Billboard* in 2015, "I don't even know who that is.")[6] But the passage of time can make a powerful case for reexamination. People are responding to *Hocus Pocus* — passionately, and in big numbers. Why? In this book, we will explore the movie's many dynamics in the hopes of figuring out why we love it so much. It just might be a finer and deeper film than even its most loyal audiences have realized. There may be more here than meets the spell book's eye.

On the topic of holiday movies, let us begin by considering that *Hocus Pocus* might appeal to us because it's as much a Christmas movie as a Halloween one — not in the literal sense of *The Nightmare Before Christmas*, but certainly in the way it approaches its holiday of choice:

> **Mrs. Olin**: We seem to have a skeptic in our midst. Mr. Dennison, would you care to give your California, laid-back, tie-dyed point of view?
>
> *The class laughs.*
>
> **Max**: Okay. Granted that you guys here in Salem are all into these black cats and witches and stuff...
>
> **Mrs. Olin**: Stuff!?
>
> *The class groans.*
>
> **Max**: Fine. But everyone here knows that Halloween was invented by the candy companies. It's a conspiracy.
>
> ❧
>
> **Dani**: Come on, Max. Couldn't you forget about being a cool teenager for one night? Please!? Come on, we used to have so much fun together trick-or-treating. Remember? It'll be like old times.
>
> **Max**: Dani, the old days are dead.
>
> ❧
>
> **Allison**: You don't like it here?
>
> **Max**: Oh, the leaves are great, but... I don't know, it's just all this Halloween stuff.
>
> **Allison**: You don't believe in it?
>
> **Max**: What do you mean, like the Sanderson sisters? No way.
>
> **Allison**: Not even on Halloween?
>
> **Max**: *Especially* not on Halloween.

In Max Dennison, we have a protagonist whose faith in Halloween is broken. "It's just a bunch of hocus pocus," he says.

What is that but a "Bah! Humbug!"?

Max is Halloween's Ebeneezer Scrooge, its Grinch, its *Miracle on 34th Street* mom. His is the classic story of a believer-turned-cynic whose shaken faith in a holiday puts him at odds with everyone around him until, through a series of extraordinary events and encounters with the supernatural, his belief is restored.[7]

By connecting us with that timeless, well-worn Christmas narrative, the movie invites to indulge in the same warm feeling of festivity we get when little Susan pulls on Santa's beard or the Grinch's heart grows three sizes in one day. It is a Christmas movie in a costume, the best trick-or-treater on the block.[8]

You best start believing in Halloween stories, Mr. Dennison. You're in one.

Like sleigh bells, Santa suits, and snow flurries in so many Christmas classics, the sights and sounds of Halloween fill the atmosphere in *Hocus Pocus*. Crisp autumn leaves crackle beneath bike paths in the cemetery lawns of Salem. Canvassed above them is a widescreen sky, varyingly cast in either deep blacks or potion-smoke purples.

Much of the movie unfolds in the night, with a very pregnant moon assuming an impossibly large portion of the frame. Jack-o'-lanterns,

Top: Ortega's vision of Halloween is suburban and idyllic, an irresisible fantasy.
Bottom: The movie's moon is a character all its own, growing larger as the plot progresses.

flickering candles, orange lights, and bales of hay flank every doorstep. Each new shot reminds us why we fell in love with the holiday as children — the mystery, the danger, the playacting, the candy, the autumn breeze whisking our hair. If Halloween were a spirit, she'd live in *Hocus Pocus*'s Salem.

Like *Home Alone*, the movie is keenly interested in finding enigma and menace in its holiday. Both stories involve home invasion. Later, we'll take a closer look at how *Hocus Pocus* hints at horror, in both its score and its narrative elements, and we might say the same of *Home Alone*. I imagine both movies make an impact, in part, because they effectively balance heartwarming sweetness with unusual peril.

Today, *Home Alone* is talked about as one of the all-time great family Christmas films. All these years later, *Hocus Pocus* is getting its due as an October counterpart. The many millions of dollars in difference between their box office receipts increasingly seem like mere trivia. Both films provide the same kinds of pleasures, and both are rich in text and subtext. As modern holiday classics, they each have a long life ahead of them, and — for those of us who've been singing *Hocus Pocus*'s praises all these years — it's a wonderful life, indeed.

Chapter Two

Make Halloween Great Again:
Jurassic Park, Nostalgia, and the Seven Gables of Salem

"Well, you see, it's like this… I… I, um… I broke into the old Sanderson house, and I brought the witches back from the dead."

W hile Max is frantically recounting his story to the phony police officer, a sign on the wall behind him comes into view, reading "House of the Seven Gables." It's the only time we see those words in the movie, but they mean more than a blurry background shot might suggest.

The house in question is a real one, first built in 1668 by a Salem sea captain and successful merchant named John Turner. Though it was a modest building at first, the Turner family expanded its footprint over the years. Reaching a final tally of three stories and 17 rooms, it became one of the largest homes of its time, an extravagant showcase of capitalist success in early America — the kind of house Max and Dani would call a trick-or-treating "jackpot." It was distinctive for its seven looming gables, each facing a different point on the compass.[1]

But when Turner's grandson squandered the family fortune, they were

The House of the Seven Gables poster appears over Max's shoulder.

forced to sell it, and in 1782, title was transferred to another captain: Samuel Ingersoll.

Samuel died at sea and left the house to his daughter, Susannah, a reclusive type who nevertheless kept in touch with her cousin, a young man named Nathaniel Hawthorne. Susannah spent her entire life in that house, a spinster, though she adopted a young boy named Horace[2] (her illegitimate child, some say) and made a handsome income off a nearby farm.

Nathaniel visited his cousin frequently, regaled by her stories of the house's history while they played cards. The Ingersolls had lopped off some of the iconic gables, but she recounted a time when all seven were still there, and it took root in Hawthorne's imagination. In particular, he was impressed by Susannah's stories about the unhappy lives of the home's former occupants, most of them long since dead, their histories mere ghosts within those walls.[3]

Later, in 1850, Hawthorne would write one of America's first and most successful mass-produced books, *The Scarlet Letter*. Its follow-up came the next year: *The House of the Seven Gables*, drawing insight out of those card-game conversations with Horace and Susannah. The novels explore themes of guilt, shame, and the social ostracizing of women. *Gables* is particularly steeped in the notion of one generation's sins revisiting the next, and it follows mysterious happenings in the house over the years, tinged with witchcraft and inexplicable manifestations of the supernatural. The characters are inspired by Susannah, her house's former dwellers, and Hawthorne's own ancestors, who had played a part in the infamous Salem Witch Trials.

Hawthorne's fame helped the house become an icon in Salem. As ownership changed hands, it was eventually restored to its many-gabled glory and turned into a museum, still running today. While primarily of interest for its literary significance and as one of New England's longest-lasting Colonial mansions, it also enjoys a reputation as a haunted house. Ghost hunters from around the country swear to have seen and even photographed the roaming spirit of Susannah Ingersoll in its halls, among a reported variety of other strange happenings there.

The house would have been 25 years old and still home to its original owners when, in *Hocus Pocus*, the Sanderson sisters abduct Emily Binx in 1693. While so much of real-world Salem colors the film's landscapes, few homes would have been not only well known but also still standing in both 1693 *and* 1993. It is no surprise, then, production designer William Sandell[4] looked to The House of the Seven Gables for inspiration when designing the movie's witchy cottage.[5]

But the mansion's long life isn't all that makes it a fitting forebear for the Sandersons. Their home, too, is a Salem house once occupied by accused witches, later turned into a museum where the unexplainable is said to have happened.

> **Allison**: Oh, you mean the Sanderson sisters?
> **Dani**: There's a museum about 'em?
> **Allison**: Yeah, but they shut it down because a lot of spooky things happened there.[6]

From the camera's vantage point, we can see only a few of the peaks in the Sandersons' roof, but it is nonetheless a "house of seven gables" in more ways than one. The fact that Salem is a town where witches really were persecuted, and where those witches' "haunted houses" really have

The Sanderson cottage is a house of many gables too.

been turned into modern-day museums, grounds the story in an unsettling historicity and an eerie nostalgia.

As *Hocus Pocus* went to theaters in the summer of 1993, it faced off against a colossal competitor at the box office: Steven Spielberg's *Jurassic Park*. (It wasn't much of a battle; *Hocus Pocus* took a venom shot to the face and was devoured alive, Newman-style.) Decades later, it's fascinating to watch the rolling tide of nostalgia come ashore for both these films, one having enjoyed a much more lucrative legacy than the other.

I couldn't help but think about *Hocus Pocus* while watching 2015's "rebootquel," *Jurassic World*.[7] In the latter, our young protagonists stumble upon the overrun and jungly remains of the original Jurassic Park, a dinosaur theme park shut down as a result of calamity before it ever got off the ground. That scene is not unlike the *Hocus Pocus* protagonists' first arrival in the Sanderson museum, thick with dust and absent of electricity, cobwebs suffocating every corner. In each, the characters are exploring the remnants of a world they'd heard of but never really known, and there is an invigorating sense of mystery in the mood.

You probably know that feeling yourself if you've ever had occasion to visit a deserted building, especially one that was open to the public, or even if you've come across pictures of long-abandoned theme parks or

Bottom: *Jurassic World (2015). Amblin Entertainment; Legendary Pictures; Dentsu; Fuji Television Network; Universal Pictures. Available from Universal Pictures Home Entertainment.*

shopping malls online.[8] We may never have visited these places for ourselves, but there is a profound sense of sadness and downright creepiness in seeing them in their discarded states.

Stories unfolded here, but we find only their aftermath. We wonder about them. New stories *could* have unfolded here, had the place not lost its sense of self, its purpose, its potential. We mourn them. And we wonder whether the places we know now might someday suffer the same fate. It is these memories and maybes — both of which elude us beyond merely a guess — that make these spaces so haunting.

The feeling is particularly potent in deserted theme parks or museums because there is something disquieting about recognizing lost (or failed) order. These are highly regimented spaces, systematic and often pristine. To see them dilapidated creates a forlornness in us — a desire for order where there is no order, a desire for people and life in a place that is now lonely and dead. It's a kind of nostalgia for histories that are not our own, not unlike the wistful feelings we might associate with eras from before our time, sometimes called "false nostalgia," though it feels just as real. In all these experiences, we face a reality in which there's something there we can't see — a history we can't know. And what is that history to us but a ghost?

In that sense, we can feel quite literally haunted by nostalgia, and so that pining makes a very powerful pairing for horror and Halloween. *Hocus Pocus* is particularly mindful about wrapping those things up in the same package. It is a film incessantly looking toward and pining for the past.

Max misses Los Angeles. Dani misses the days when her brother eagerly took her trick-or-treating. Thackery misses his sister. The Sandersons miss their youth, their good looks, and their mother. For all of them, Halloween isn't what it used to be.

"Sisters," Winifred cries, "All Hallows' Eve has become a night of frolic, where children wear costumes and run amok."

Even Allison's parents are looking back to the past, their annual Colonial-themed Halloween party a nod to the same time period in which The House of the Seven Gables was built. We might even read their scene as a foreshadow: Allison thinks she's ditching the 1600s when she sneaks out of the house, but little does she know that the 1600s aren't quite done with her yet. Indeed, it isn't just witches who have come to terrorize Salem. It's the town's past.

Nostalgia has been an important part of *Hocus Pocus*'s resurgence in popularity (though, as we will see in *Chapter 13*, not the only part). Undoubtedly, we can feel sentimental toward many things for many reasons all at once, but I wonder if one of the reasons we feel such fierce nostalgia toward *Hocus Pocus* is that the characters feel it themselves. Does the movie invite us to join them in wishing Halloween could be like it once was? Is Halloween, with all its ties to childhood and its invocations of the dead, inextricably bound up in nostalgia for us?

The thing about nostalgia is it can only be fleetingly quenched. We can never return to the past, but for brief stretches of time, it can return to us. And so we re-rent favorite movies, line up at museums, and clamor for sequels steeped in reminiscence.

Somehow, the Halloweens ahead of us are made better by the ones we've lived in our past. And so *Hocus Pocus* grows dearer to us with each passing year. It's the kind of sentiment Winifred expresses when she looks out on the early-A.M. hours and cries, "Another glorious morning... makes me sick!" Nostalgia is bittersweet.

The march of time means we are always moving further away from the Halloweens we cherished. But in that same traipse, we find our affection for them grows. Part of the "magic" of the movies is their ability to transport. You needn't have grown up with *Hocus Pocus* for it to remind you of your youth. To some extent, the childhood experience of Halloween is universal, and the movie is constantly capturing and recapturing it, no matter how old we get.

Chapter Three

Spielberg's Second-Best Halloween Movie

What's your favorite Steven Spielberg movie, and why is it *Hocus Pocus*? Before you run to look at the back of your Blu-ray in disbelief, let me clarify: Steven Spielberg[1] didn't direct *Hocus Pocus*, nor does his name appear anywhere in the closing credits. Conventionally speaking, this is a Kenny Ortega movie. He's the director, after all, and if there's one thing we're taught about movies, it's that directors "make" them. But isn't *Hocus Pocus* as much "a Disney movie" and "a Bette Midler movie"[2] as an Ortega one?

With books, we talk about authors. With movies, we talk about *auteurs*, mostly because people with film degrees leap at the chance to speak French. An auteur (pronounced like author without the h, essentially) is defined as "a filmmaker whose personal influence or artistic control over a movie are so great that the filmmaker is regarded as the movie's author."[3] In the early days of film studies, conventional wisdom held that directors were always the auteurs, and their movies should be analyzed accordingly. That's called "Auteur Theory," and it can sometimes prove illuminating. But movies are collaborative projects, and while directors often *are* the most distinctive voices in their films, there are plenty of screenwriters, actors, producers, and cinematographers who've emerged as auteurs in their own right — artists whose distinctive styles overpower even the director's. Incidentally, there is no finer example than Walt Disney himself, the ultimate non-directorial auteur.

A Kenny Ortega Movie

In full disclosure, I am a Kenny Ortega fan. As this book goes to press, the man has directed only eight movies, four of which were made for television. That's not a lot to go on, but those movies include *Newsies*, *High School Musical*, and of course, *Hocus Pocus*. Sold. Do I even need to mention he directed and designed Michael Jackson's most epic tours, beginning with *Dangerous* in 1992 and continuing through the theatrical release of *This Is It*[4] in 2009?

Ortega, though, is better known to Hollywood for his work as a choreographer, which began under the tutelage of Gene Kelly[5] on the set of *Xanadu* in 1979-80 (*quite* a mentor). He went on to create the cadence of the '80s in films like *Dirty Dancing*, *St. Elmo's Fire*, and *Pretty in Pink*, not to mention the music video for Madonna's "Material Girl."[6] In the 1990s, he helmed Super Bowl halftime shows, world tours for Gloria Estefan and Cher, and high-profile performances at the Olympics and the Academy Awards. In the Aughts, he enjoyed a stint as Miley Cyrus's choreographer during her explosive "Hannah Montana" days and, more recently, one-off directorial turns on shows like "Bunheads" and "Crazy Ex-Girlfriend."

At the box office, though, his directorial projects have been less successful. Neither *Newsies* nor *Hocus Pocus* made much money. His biggest claim to fame would come years later on The Disney Channel with *High School Musical* and *Descendants*.

In studying the Ortega filmography, we can find at least a few trends: youthful protagonists, iconic actresses, an affinity for song-and-dance sequences, epic-scale film sets (wherever budgets allow for it), and abundant camp. And a fascinating thing happens with Ortega movies — they meet apathy and/or derision upon release and then become veritable phenomena.

In terms of *Hocus Pocus*, the most interesting cross-reference in the Ortega oeuvre may very well be Michael Jackson's "Thriller." Remember: he was staging the *Dangerous* tour around the same time he directed *Hocus Pocus*, and he later helped bring "Thriller" to new life in a Haunted Mansion-inspired music video remake. In all these things, it's clear he has a keen ability to communicate the thrill of Halloween visually. *Hocus Pocus* is optically lush, and that is undoubtedly a testament to Ortega as a visionary.

But conventional auteur theory works best when a director has a very large body of work. Critics wouldn't ordinarily look at Ortega as an auteur; he's simply better known for his work outside the director's chair. Accordingly, we might gleam some additional insight by casting conventional auteur theory aside and thinking outside the box, looking at other parties as additional "auteurs" (with sincerest respect for Mr. Ortega, of course).[7]

A Disney Movie

Earlier, we considered the idea that producers can be auteurs. In terms of filmmaking, Walt Disney's chief claim to fame was as producer. Nearly all his projects were made with someone else in the director's chair, yet still, we tend to think of those as "Disney movies" — the directors are mostly unknown to the masses.

What if we go a step further and think of the company Walt left behind as an auteur as well? Disney might be the *only* major modern Hollywood studio functioning as an auteur in its own right. Neither Paramount, Warner, Sony, Fox, nor Universal so consistently produce films of a similar mold, and none of those companies have carved out an authorial style as identifiable as Disney's.[8] I dare say audiences could more readily single out a film as being "like Disney" than "like Sony" or "like Fox." What would it even mean for a movie to be "like a Sony movie" today?

Incidentally, one of the chief arguments in my *Thinking Fan's Guide to Walt Disney World* books is that Disney theme parks excel largely because the public understands "Disney" to mean something in terms of narrative and moral value, whereas other studios' names are essentially just logos.

But what constitutes a Disney movie, exactly? And is *Hocus Pocus* one?

(Setting aside the obvious fact that the company did indeed produce it.) Here, the problem is opposite of the Ortega oeuvre — there are *so many* Disney movies that an effort to identify the common trends can seem overwhelming. But let's give it a shot: magic, musical numbers, talking animals, larger-than-life and visually striking villains, a focus on the family (despite the relative absence of one or more parents), intertextuality[9], and happy endings. *Hocus Pocus* checks every box.

In it, we find the same alluring tone of whimsical good-naturedness that imbues so many Disney films. It's a genial blend of action, adventure, comedy, sentiment, and occasional sadness, with a sense of humor that knocks on corny's door but never quite goes inside — heavy on heart but not heavyhearted. Like any person with those same traits would be, the blend is immensely winsome.

A Disney film is nothing if not an underscoring of wholesome values, or at least values that have been normalized as wholesome. And while *Hocus Pocus* is edgier than most (a fact we'll dive headfirst into later), the ultimate takeaway is quintessentially Disney: the world is a supernatural place, and good triumphs over evil in the end.

A Spielberg Movie

Here's where we *really* start thinking outside the box. If Walt Disney can be an auteur as producer, and if the studio he left behind can in turn become an auteur because it emulates his style, is it possible for an influential artist to become a movie's "auteur" even if he or she never works on it?

For instance, given that it was created by many of Disney's people and in the Disney style, might it be fair to think of *Chitty Chitty Bang Bang* as a Disney movie, even though it technically isn't one? We can put up the same question for *Hocus Pocus*: might it be "a Spielberg movie" even if he never had an official role in the cast or crew?

Lest it seem we're grasping for straws, consider this: *Hocus Pocus* was very nearly a Spielberg movie in the literal sense. Once the decision was made to move it from television to theaters, creator and producer David Kirschner[10] pitched the project to Spielberg and asked him to direct or, if nothing else, at least come on board as producer. He was interested. Everything about the script was right up his alley circa 1993 — it is spirited, adventurous, wide-eyed, fantastical, family-oriented, and tinged with fear. And he liked Kirschner, who had created the characters and stories for Spielberg's *An American Tail* (1986). Mick Garris[11] was in the mix too, another plus. At the same time he was developing *Hocus Pocus* with Kirschner, Garris was also a writer and director for Spielberg's "Amazing Stories" on NBC.

Accounts differ as to why Spielberg ultimately declined. Garris and journalist Tim Greiving have both suggested the decision was a matter of loyalty.[12] (Spielberg was wrapped up in his own production company, Amblin, which soured in its relationship with Disney after *Who Framed Roger Rabbit* in 1988, and he launched a rival animation house soon thereafter.) Either way, the project went full steam ahead without him, and Disney attached Midler and Ortega along the way.[13]

Still, "Spielberg pixie dust" doesn't shake off easily.[14] Here is a movie written, developed, and initially scored by Spielberg collaborators, and all with the famed director in mind at one point or another. In fact, Spielberg even spent time on the *Hocus Pocus* set, visiting Walt Disney Studios Stage 2, home to the elaborate Sanderson cottage and water wheel. While the extent of his contributions there (if any) remain a mystery, there *is* an especially Spielbergian scope and grandeur to that set and its presentation on film.

As adjectives go, "Spielbergian" isn't a bad one for *Hocus Pocus*. So-called "serious" critics often look at whether non-Hitchcock films are "Hitchcockian," so why not engage in that same line of thought where the Blockbuster King is concerned?[15]

In the early days, Spielberg's reputation was that of "the big kid with a camera." He brings a childlike sense of wonder to the lens. And more often than not, children become his stars. His cinematic fantasies are driven by mysticism, rooted in suburbia, and built around broken families. They are deep in emotion and sophisticated in cinematography.

With those traits, the director carved out a subset of the blockbuster: the 1980s-90s family fantasy-adventure.[16] So many of the movies from that era evidence a decidedly Spielbergian sensibility: *Honey, I Shrunk the*

Kids; *Jumanji*; *Home Alone*; and more.

Hocus Pocus stands tall among them. Its script flings children into a terrifying ordeal, the resolution of which repairs a rift in the family. The score is spirited, mysterious, and memorable. Its cinematography prizes scope and conveys a sense of awe. You're almost waiting for E.T. and Elliott to dart across that bullion moon on the horizon.

Granted, if Spielberg *had* taken hold of the camera, we'd likely have something less colorful and campy than Kenny Ortega's product — a slightly artsier film with a smidgen more restraint. Incidentally, we'd also have a second Spielberg story set at Halloween.

Mind you, were *Hocus Pocus* literally a Spielberg film, I wouldn't dare rank it atop *E.T.*, his original Halloween masterpiece, widely considered a definitive benchmark. But then, I wager that within the Spielberg oeuvre, second place isn't such a bad score. And truth be told, if Spielberg's name had been attached all along, critics might not have given *Hocus Pocus* such a bad score either.[17]

Chapter Four

The Divine Miss Sanderson

Bette Midler was an unlikely Mickey Mouse.

With *Ruthless People* and *Down and Out in Beverly Hills* in 1986, the bawdy star became the face of a brand-new studio label: Touchstone Pictures, Disney's effort to enter the R-rated movie market without tarnishing its late Uncle Walt's family-friendly name. The movies were huge hits, and Disney was suddenly walking arm in arm with a star whose act would never have played on Main Street, U.S.A.

Even before she was making R-rated comedies, here was the woman who in 1972 turned Bobby Freeman's sweet "Do You Want to Dance" into a sultry heavy breather of a ballad, wherein "dance" now meant something else altogether, and whose second moniker had always been "Bathhouse Betty."[1] She had a reputation for ribaldry but also for talent — the multi-hyphenate kind (actor, singer, dancer, comedienne, star of Broadway, and the list goes on). When Michael Eisner left Paramount to assume the CEO spot at The Walt Disney Company in 1984, he hadn't brought any sense of "Jiminy Cricket" with him. He cared about good scripts and bankable talent, and in Midler, he saw a vehicle for both. And as it happened, she needed a ride too.

Disney was the second wind beneath Bette Midler's wings. Her big screen debut in *The Rose* (1979) had been embraced as a revelation, earning her an Oscar nomination and a Golden Globe for Best Actress.[2] But film offers didn't follow, so she went back to what made her famous in the first place, music and touring. It wasn't until she teamed up with Eisner in the mid-1980s that she became a major movie star.

A string of Touchstone films followed, nearly all of them rated PG-13 or R: *Outrageous Fortune* (1987), *Beaches* (1988), *Stella* (1990), and *Scenes from a Mall* (1991).[3] By the early '90s, she had emerged as one of Disney's biggest players and a universally beloved household name — brassy and over the top but consistently fun.

Even she was surprised by her ascension as headmistress of the Mouse House. A reporter asked about her improbable home in the hallowed halls of Disney in 1988.

"Ironic, ain't it?" she quipped. "But I loved Disney's view of the world, even though it was a narrow one. It did a service, yet a disservice, too. Let's face it: if Walt Disney were alive today, they wouldn't let me in the front gate of the studio."[4]

Her history as headliner for Disney's saucy side makes it easier to understand how *Hocus Pocus* became arguably the edgiest thing ever released with Walt Disney's name attached. In some sense, by 1993, "Bette Midler" had come to mean "Disney on the edge." Audiences knew she wasn't one to shy away from the licentious. Another actress might not have afforded *Hocus Pocus* the creative license to boldly go where family films usually don't.[5]

The Bette Midler "brand" circa 1993 highlights how fitting a choice she was for the *movie*. But there is an even more fundamental quality in Midler that made her right for the *role*.

Winifred Sanderson is a witch from three hundred years ago, and Bette Midler has always been a blast from the past herself — an old-school musical trio wrapped up in one woman, the Andrews Sisters meet Mae West. In 2014, she released a new collection of iconic "girl group" covers spanning seven decades, *It's the Girls!*, and it broke records.[6] The album was lauded for getting to the very essence of who Bette Midler is as an artist.

From her showbiz debut as one of the "Matchmaker" sisters in *Fiddler on the Roof* to her first Top Ten pop single (a cover of the World War II anthem, "Boogie Woogie Bugle Boy") and her enormously successful collaboration with Diane Keaton and Goldie Hawn in *The First Wives Club*'s "You Don't Own Me," Midler has made herself a final flag-waver for girl-group entertainments of yore.[7] So when she shows up in *Hocus Pocus* as a larger-than-life lead singer in a trio of sister witches brought back from the past, she brings with her the stamp of an artist from a different mold and a different time.

During press for *Hocus Pocus* in 1993, she described how thrilling it felt to perform in a three-women comedy act, long a secret ambition. Winifred allowed her to live out that fantasy in a musical troupe of comediennes, the Three Stooges of Salem. It's no wonder she calls this her favorite film role to date, beaming with pride whenever a reporter asks. Winifred was wish fulfillment — a kind of Disney dream come true, where the princess is a diva and a double-humped mop of red hair is her crown.

> "I have to tell you about Halloween... The reason I love Halloween so much is because I made possibly the greatest Halloween movie *ever*. I mean, there are only six of them, and mine I think is at least number one or number two. It was *Hocus Pocus*, which they play incessantly, which I feel is my *finest* hour. I feel it's my finest hour."[8]

Each of the three witch actresses was allowed to create her character from whole cloth. Midler went where the thrust of her personality compelled her to go, concocting a kind of Norma Desmond for the devil, with just a dash of Cruella DeVil, the Queen of Hearts, and the Marx Brothers' Margaret Dumont.[9]

When I found out Chris Azzopardi was interviewing The Divine One in advance of *It's the Girls!*, I suggested he ask whether she'd consider "I Put a Spell on You" for the accompanying tour.

"After all," I wondered, "aren't the Sanderson sisters really a girl group?

And, for that matter, The First Wives too?" Chris, an acquaintance of mine and something of a superstar himself in the world of celebrity journalism, kindly obliged.

"I really do have to think about this," Midler answered. "If I go out around Halloween, I'll have to put some effort into it. I've got some surprises up my sleeve."[10] Far be it from me to claim credit for either of us, but sure enough, the tour hit the road with Midler's first-ever live performance of "I Put a Spell on You" built in. I bet she couldn't wait.

That song isn't just up her sleeve; it's in her soul. In Winifred, Bette Midler finds an *alter ego*. And in *Hocus Pocus*, she finds a *magnum opus*.

Chapter Five

Everything's Coming Up Winnie:
The Why of Her Whammy in "I Put a Spell on You"

"**I** put a spell on you... now you're gone... my hardest spell on you... it was strong."

For about 22 years, I thought those were the words in Winifred Sanderson's version of "I Put a Spell on You." Imagine my surprise when, one Halloween, I overheard a friend singing, "My whammy fell," not "my hardest spell."

"Ummm... what did you just say?" I asked, cockily and incredulously. "Those are *not* the words." I was very Lucy van Pelt about it.

After all, I'm no fly-by-night *Hocus Pocus* fan. The idea that I'd been walking around singing this song (as grown men do) incorrectly all these years did not agree with me.

Well, as it turns out, I was wrong. Even after hearing it in various theme park productions and sitting a hundred feet from Ms. Midler performing it live, I'd somehow missed the memo.

You see, when Winifred sings it, she's nearly silent with the "w" in "whammy." I guess my little-boy brain picked up the "h" sound and heard "hardest" (not a bad lyric, if I do say so myself), and I'd never looked back.

But now I'm in a whole new world of revelation. It's Winnie's whammy that falls on the crowd, only Bette says it more like "hammy," which hits the nail on the head because she is chewing that scenery *up*!

"Whammy" is a word with many meanings: bad luck, the evil eye, or a devastating blow. But in its oldest and most literal sense, a "whammy" is a magical spell, and specifically a jinx or a curse. Since that's exactly what this song is when the Sandersons sing it, the lyric is oh so apropos.

But the song didn't originate with *Hocus Pocus*, and in its first life, "whammy" wasn't one of the words. For that matter, most of Midler's phraseology is new.

It originated in 1956 with opera singer-turned-R&B rock-and-roller Jay Hawkins... or Screamin' Jay Hawkins, as he became known in the immediate aftermath of "I Put a Spell on You."

If you've never heard the original, it is... *something*. The opening riff lustily lurches in like a hot-to-trot Frankenstein's monster. Then Hawkins starts to sing... well, wail, really, but he's reasonably restrained enough for the first 15 seconds or so. Then he breaks into a fit of deranged laughter and two minutes of gasping, growling, howling, snorting, and snarling. It's unsettling, provocative, and overflowing with real soul. Good stuff.

Hawkins had intended to record a serious, stately love song. In his version of the lyric, he hopes desperately for a spell that will fix his love's wandering eyes on him and him alone. It was going to be beautiful. But then his producer showed up with a bunch of booze. Wild and wasted, Hawkins gave us a recording that *rocked* rock and roll.

Though it's usually packaged as a novelty song these days, "I Put a Spell on You" was a sensation at the time. It launched the "shock rock" subgenre all on its own, paving the way for Alice Cooper, Ozzy Osbourne, and Marilyn Manson. Screamin' Jay embraced his new persona with full abandon — capes, canes, snakes, skulls, cigarette-smoking skeletons, tusks in his nose — the works. He even arrived on stage in a coffin. His newfound flare for the theatrical propelled the rest of his career (and helped him fare pretty well with the ladies... Hawkins fathered as many as 75 children during his 70 years on Earth.) Incidentally, he also influenced blues singer Dr. John, who later provided the music for Disney's *The Princess and the Frog.* The animators for that film reportedly based its villain, Dr. Facilier, on the one and only Screamin' Jay.

Years later, the Rock and Roll Hall of Fame inducted the recording as one of "500 Songs That Shaped Rock and Roll," and *Rolling Stone* magazine named it one of "The 500 Greatest Songs of All Time." By then, it had been covered frequently, a tradition that continues to this day. Notable renditions include those by Annie Lenox, Creedence Clearwater Revival, Queen Latifah, Nina Simone, She & Him, and Jeff Beck with Joss Stone, among others. Its individual elements have been sampled in everything from jazz (Frank Sinatra's "The World We Knew") to acid house (Legion of Dynamic Diskord's "Rebel Rebel") to rap (The Notorious B.I.G.'s "Kick in the Door").

Suffice it to say *Hocus Pocus* takes a different approach. The underlying riff is only barely there, and the lyrics are almost entirely new. Here, it's a much jazzier affair, with a shot of show tune and a pinch of pop-rock for good measure.

Musically, you might say Bette Midler travels in six lanes: Broadway (*Gypsy; Hello, Dolly!*), pop ("From a Distance"), doo-wop (the girl groups discussed in the previous chapter), rock and roll ("Beast of Burden," *The Rose*), the standard ("Come Rain or Come Shine"), and easy listening/ vocal jazz ("In the Mood").[1] Those roads intersect at the Salem Town Hall, where Winifred Sanderson enchants the hapless parents of Massachusetts's North Shore with one spell of a showstopper.

It's Bette unbridled, over the top and larger than life, as only the best Disney villains are. In less capable hands, it might have gone gauche, but this is the Divine Miss M, and no one wants a milder Midler. Besides, even in its earliest days, "I Put a Spell on You" was performance art. By Screamin' Jay standards, Winifred is practically perched on a stool and strumming a ukulele.

For both Hawkins and *Hocus,* the song is ultimately about its singer trying to gain control. But for Winifred, it might be about even more than that.

At this point, it's helpful to ask ourselves whether *Hocus Pocus* is a movie musical or just "a movie with musical moments." Generally speaking, if movie characters break into song and dance, we call it a musical. But when Audrey Hepburn sings "Moon River" in *Breakfast at Tiffany's*, Joseph Gordon-Levitt bursts into a highly choreographed ensemble dance sequence in *(500) Days of Summer*, or John Travolta twists with Uma Thurman in *Pulp Fiction*, we accept those scenes merely as "moments" (even though each of those actors is associated with movie musicals elsewhere).

The distinction probably has something to do with quantity. It's easier to call a movie a musical when it has fifteen songs rather than one. But what about a movie with only two songs? Three? Four? Where do we draw the line?

In place of a numerical definition, we can dig a little deeper and ask how the songs are used within the story.

Musical performances in non-musicals tend to *interrupt* the narrative. In other words, they are designed to affect the audience by surprising them with something excessive, unexpected, or unlike the rest of the film.[2] Gordon-Levitt's "just-got-laid" jig is effective, for example, because it happens in a movie where spontaneous dance is not the norm. Alternatively, the songs may be mostly *incidental* to the story, as in *Sister Act* (1992).

On the contrary, movie musical numbers *engage* the narrative. They are used to shed light on a scene, reflect on the story, or develop a character's emotional plight. The characters themselves *achieve* something by singing too, whether it's getting an emotion out of their systems or hashing out a dilemma.[3]

There isn't always a clear divide. We could describe nearly every Bette Midler movie, for example, as a "movie with musical moments." Aside from concert films, she's made surprisingly few full-fledged musicals for an actor of her theatrical abilities: *For the Boys*, *Oliver & Company*, *Gypsy*, and arguably *The Rose*. But she sings at least one song in *Jinxed*, *Big Business*, *Beaches*, *Stella*, *Scenes from a Mall*, *The First Wives Club*, *That Old Feeling*, and *Isn't She Great*, none of which are generally considered musicals. The math speaks for itself: if Bette Midler's in the lead, she's probably going to sing. And in those cases, the function of the song might have less to do with disrupting or engaging the narrative than with simply appeasing the actress's fan base. A Bette Midler movie with no singing would be like an Adele concert with no "Rolling in the Deep." Like, really, Adele? C'mon.

Never fear; *Hocus Pocus* doesn't disappoint. The Divine Miss M sings several times, and she isn't even the only one. So does that make it a musical?

My Name's Winifred! What's Yours?

If I asked you how many songs are in the movie, you'd probably tell me two: "Garden of Magic" and "I Put a Spell on You." Actually, there are four others with lyrics: an untitled a cappella song (performed by the witches during their hanging); "Chants and Incantations" (the spell that turns Thackery into a cat — rhythmic, certainly, and officially credited as a song, but not very melodic); "Witchcraft" (the skeleton band's abridged cover of the Frank Sinatra song); and "Row, Row, Row Your Boat" (performed briefly by Ice and Jay). One might even consider Mary and Sarah's "Remember, Winnie, Remember" a musical moment. But "I Put a Spell on You" stands out as especially theatrical.

Right off the bat, the song invites us to think of it as a musical number. After a campy spoken-word preamble ("Thank you, Max, for that *marvelous* introduction"), our star takes the stage with "Hello, Salem! My name's Winifred! What's yours?"

The line is an allusion to "Rose's Turn," considered by many to be the greatest song by the greatest character in the greatest stage musical of all time: 1959's *Gypsy*, written by Jule Styne and Stephen Sondheim.[4]

When one musical references another, scholars call it "intertexuality." That happens in other genres too (and especially on shows like "The Simpsons" and "Family Guy"), but it's especially common in musicals, given that so many of them involve adaptations of previous works. Academics like to look for the "why" of the intertextual reference. What is it telling us? What does it add to our understanding of the story?

Gypsy is the story of Mama Rose, who raised real-life striptease artist Gypsy Rose Lee and became the ultimate stage mom, relentlessly projecting her ambitious dreams of stardom onto her daughters. Toward the end of Act II, realizing her star has passed her by, Rose unleashes a lifetime of resentment and regret in a spectacular tour-de-force. Peppered with stuttering asides and non-sequiturs, it is essentially a nervous breakdown in the form of a song. At one point, she addresses an empty theater and shouts, "Hello, everybody! My name's Rose! What's yours?" [5]

That "Rose's Turn" turns up in *Hocus Pocus* is interesting for a few reasons. Among them: Bette Midler would win a Golden Globe for singing that song in a highly acclaimed TV adaptation of *Gypsy* later in the very same year, 1993. [6]

Narratively, the song is doing three things at once. From the perspective of Salem's parents, the Sandersons are a local novelty act, a part of the show. So when Winifred gets up there and breaks into a song about magic, she's just being cheeky. It's a ruse, and they fall for it. But from Winifred's perspective, this is all very literal — she really is casting a spell, and she's singing as herself, in the first person. Meanwhile, from our perspective as audience members, the spontaneous arrival of song and dance tells us something different is happening in the movie. We might be inclined to think of it as just another one of Midler's "musical moments," but the *Gypsy* reference invites us to think of it in terms of musical theatre instead.

In "Rose's Turn," Mama Rose lets loose because she just *has* to get it out of her. "With what I've been holding down inside of me," she cries, "if I ever let it out, there wouldn't be signs big enough! ...Lights bright enough! ...Here she is, world! Heeeeere's ROSE!"

Is the eldest Sanderson having a Rose moment of her own here? Does Winnie just *have* to get this out of her? Does Bette?

For us, part of the thrill in this scene is that it's "Midler to the max," a spectacular showcase of talent. And inasmuch as this is an explosion of a character's emotion, it is very much a movie musical sequence. [7]

Domineering, arrogant, and condescending, Winifred is as overbearing a sister as Rose is a mom. Both women shout their "Hello!" in their second stage of life. For Mama Rose, it's vicarious stardom through her daughter. For Winifred, it's resurrection after being hanged. They're both desperate and in their last hurrahs. And they both have a mother complex too. Repeatedly, Rose stops to stammer, "Momma? ...Momma?" but nobody

Top: Bette Midler as Mama Rose, performing "Rose's Turn" in Gypsy *(1993). RHI Entertainment, Inc.; Sonar Entertainment; CBS. Available from Mill Creek Home Entertainment.*

is there. Winnie asks, "What would Mother say?" And twice, she and her sisters stop to face the sky and sigh, "Mother."

By the end, Rose has convinced herself she'll come out on top yet. "Everything's coming up Rose," she sings, "...everything's coming up roses, this time, for me." Winnie leaves her scene newly assured of victory too. "Dance until you die!" she tells the crowd, making her exit with an evil cackle the newly bewitched townsfolk fail to register.

A Musical en Vogue

Winnie's dancing-death spell nods to more than just *Gypsy*. Madonna's "Vogue" comes into play too, as Mrs. Dennison performs the iconic dance while costumed as the pop star.[8]

A few observations become immediately apparent. In "Vogue," Madonna namechecks two people of significance to *Hocus Pocus*: Gene Kelly (the man who helped Kenny Ortega get his start in show biz) and Bette Davis (Midler was named after her). Even more to the point, lyrically, "Vogue" can be read as a kind of dance spell in and of itself, calling its audience to surrender against struggle and give in to the dance. There's a sense of futility in lines like "you try everything you can to escape," "when all else fails... get out on the dance floor," and "let your body move to the music." The lyrics even refer to dancing as "magical."

The camera cuts to Mrs. Dennison voguing right as Winifred exclaims, "Dance until you die," the iconic moves providing visual affirmation that Mrs. Dennison and the rest of the crowd are now slaves to the music.

The audiences of 1993, though, weren't nearly so beguiled by the stylings of Broadway on the big screen. Movie musicals had been on the decline for some time, and interestingly enough, film historian John Kenneth Muir blames two films for putting the final nails in the coffin: Ortega's *Newsies* and Midler's *For the Boys*, both of which had been enormous box office flops in 1991-92.[9] It's probably no surprise, then, so many moviegoers dismissed this scene as silly in 1993. That was the general consensus for all movie musicals. They'd become overwrought, superfluous, and passé.

But there was one last bastion for the musical in Hollywood: the animated

Mama Rose: "Strike a pose."

feature. Whereas the live-action, big-screen musical had died, Disney's hand-drawn musicals were roaring back to life. Audiences of all ages embraced films such as *The Little Mermaid* (1989), *Beauty and the Beast* (1991), and *Aladdin* (1992), but the rap with grown-ups was that musical outbursts ought to be left for cartoons.

The kids of that era, though, wouldn't have had so clear a sense of separation. Ensemble showstoppers were the soundtrack of their generation. When the Sandersons took to the stage for a rousing musicale, they were speaking the language of the '90s kids.

Showtunes-weary moviegoers might have kicked the bucked beneath the movie's noose, then, but the sisters' whammy worked — some twenty-five years later, *Hocus Pocus* is back from the dead, and those now-grown children celebrate the song instead. Everything's coming up Winnie, after all.

Chapter Six

Gardeners of Magic:
James Horner, John Debney, and Sarah Jessica Parker

Ranking the ways in which *Hocus Pocus* is underrated would be about as easy as catching the Golden Snitch on an Oreck upright. But nothing grinds my gears quite so much as when its score, a real Firebolt, gets disregarded like the Weasley twins' Cleansweep Fives.

As with so many great works, the movie's music grew out of a creative crisis and an impending deadline. Composers aren't usually involved with a film until after shooting has wrapped, coming in sometime around the editing stage. But exceptions are made when the actors need to be "diegetically aware" (in other words, the music will come from within their universe, so they need to respond to it on-screen). Since Sarah Jessica Parker was to sing as Sarah Sanderson, scorer James Horner would need to come in early and write at least that one song.

Horner already enjoyed a reputation as one of Hollywood's most accomplished composers, coming off a recent string of family films that included *The Rocketeer*; *Honey, I Shrunk the Kids*; *Once Upon a Forest*; and *An American Tail*. He was a big get for *Hocus Pocus*, secured in part because of his work with Spielberg and Kirschner.

But Horner stuck around just long enough to compose four cues: two for Sarah's song ("Garden of Magic"), one for pre-feline Thackery's jaunt into the woods, and a very brief piece called "Winnie Wants Children." When a sudden scheduling conflict pulled Horner away at the last minute, Disney had to scramble. The orchestra was already set to record in two weeks, and they only had about five minutes' worth of music written.

In a pickle, the studio called on a relatively untested composer named John Debney to fill Horner's shoes. Weighing in his favor: he was available. He'd also earned *beaming* recommendations from both Kirschner and Horner, and despite his relatively meager filmography at the time, he was no stranger to the Mouse.

Louis Debney, John's father, had been working with Walt Disney since the early days of Donald Duck. Louis cut his teeth as a clapper boy[1] and production assistant on Mickey cartoons and *Snow White and the Seven Dwarfs*, and in later years, as an associate producer and supervisor on "Disneyland," "Zorro," the "Mickey Mouse Club," and a handful of live-action feature films, including *The Adventures of Bullwhip Griffin* and *Babes in Toyland*. A self-labeled "Disney brat," the junior Debney grew up on the Disney lot, hobnobbing with the Sherman Brothers and watching his dad at work. Fresh out of college, Debney did some small-scale work for Disney, nabbing "additional music" credits on a handful of TV productions while also working outside the studio for "Star Trek: The Next Generation" and Hanna-Barbera. He had even contributed music to a few Disney theme park attractions, including EPCOT Center's entrance medley and the Horizons ride, as well as Magic Kingdom's unforgettable SpectroMagic parade.

Horner's exit opened a door for Debney to create his first major motion picture score. You can imagine the pressure: he was young, it was his first big gig, he was taking over from one of the biggest names in Hollywood, major movie stars were in the picture, and he had *two weeks* to write the whole thing. But boy, did he deliver.

Writing during the day and conducting a 92-piece orchestra at night, Debney crafted one of the most spirited and enveloping film compositions of the 1990s. He invited a choir to add eeriness to its atmosphere, like the air itself were in awe of what it found in Salem. You can nearly hear color in the melodies — crimson violets, crisp and leafy browns, and hues of mossy green and orange in the ambience, as though "earth tones" were a reference not to color but to wind and sound. Pocahontas would be proud.

The main title, which also opens the film, begins with a vocal "ahhhhh," like the glorious reveal of long-lost treasure, set atop an ominous blend of flute, music box, and chimes. It starts soft but suspenseful, the strings slowly working themselves into a beehived frenzy. Then there's a cymbal clash, and the track absolutely *explodes*. Brass blares while bells knell funereally. Like overlords, the trumpets pitch evil orders to the strings, which carry them out in fever-pitched obedience. Woodwinds leap for the sky. The instruments become wildebeest, stampeding with such pace the listener feels swept up in an extremely dangerous adventure. It's wicked adrenaline. For my money, this is as exciting as contemporary film score gets.

Debney's vision was for a soundtrack that balanced the film's silliness against its more sinister side, creating an undercurrent of mystery and peril.

"I never wanted to make it so light that it would be farcical," he said. "I wanted to make sure the music could be magical and witchlike and elegant and rich, but my feeling was if it were too comedic, you'd let the air out of it."[2] The balancing act calls Disney's Haunted Mansion and Pirates of the Caribbean to mind, though *Hocus Pocus* is probably even more menacing in tone. (Incidentally, Debney is responsible for the spooky score in Disneyland Paris's Phantom Manor, a more macabre take on the stateside Mansion.)

Two other Debney themes help define the film. "Meeting Allison" is bouncy and effervescent at first, beautifully capturing the childlike charm of trick-or-treating. But it soon eases into a heartwarming, easy-tempered love theme, ever so slightly reminiscent of the gorgeous "Gabriel's Oboe" from Ennio Morricone's score for *The Mission* (1986).

Of course, there are two loves in Max's life, and his budding romance with Allison isn't the only relationship with an anthem. Even lusher, "Max and Dani" exudes the gentle warmth that defined the 1990s live-action family adventure film.

Out of those three themes emerges the film's prevailing sentiment, an endearing blend of fight-or-flight urgency, sibling harmony, and young love, all of it emotionally potent.

Debney drew inspiration from Paul Dukas's *The Sorcerer's Apprentice* (popularized in Walt Disney's *Fantasia*) and John Williams's *The Witches of Eastwick*. Both influences are as apparent as they are welcome. At other times his work here is reminiscent of Danny Elfman's theme for *Batman* (1989), Rimsky-Korsakov's famous "Flight of the Bumblebee," and the soundtrack for *The Addams Family* (1991, scored by none other than Marc Shaiman, who also arranged "I Put a Spell on You" and many of Midler's other projects).[3] Meanwhile, in the "Black Candle" cue, he makes musical reference to Miss Gulch's theme from *The Wizard of Oz* (1939).

Two other pieces of classical music make their way into the soundtrack. Mozart's *Divertimento No. 17 in D Major, K. 334* sets the mood for the Colonial-themed and clearly humdrum Halloween soiree at Allison's house (ain't no party like a Mozart party 'cause a Mozart party don't start). Later, Mary goes mental over a zany baby ad on TV. Set to the hectic melody of Aram Khachaturian's "Sabre Dance," the DuPont Stainmaster carpet commercial is a real one that ran in the early '90s, and it had become something of a pop culture in-joke by 1993. It's one of the funniest bits in the film, and Kathy Najimy nails it with one outlandish shriek. (By the way, can we all take a moment to appreciate that the vacuum-riding witch is the one who gets a kick out of the carpet commercial?)

Despite its grandeur, *Hocus Pocus* never got a proper soundtrack release. Debney circulated a handful of promotional copies at the time, but they were almost instantly scarce. I still remember walking into Media Play and asking for the soundtrack a few years later ("CD or cassette will be fine"). The employee looked on this new thing called the internet and explained the situation to me. For the next decade, I would ask literally every record store I ever stepped foot in if they had a copy. Eventually, in the Aughts, a widely disseminated bootleg fell in my lap... not ideal, but better than nothing for this hungry *Hocus Pocus* fan. Finally, in 2013, an independent film-score preservationist label by the name of Intrada worked with Disney and Debney to release *Hocus Pocus: Original Motion Picture Soundtrack* on CD at long last.[4]

The only lyrical recording on the soundtrack is Sarah Jessica Parker's — not an easy song to name. Online, people call it "Come, Little Children." Officially, though, it's "Garden of Magic," and it appears twice: first as instrumental accompaniment while Sarah lures Emily to her cottage and then again when Parker sings it aboard her broom. To avoid confusion, Intrada calls the earlier cue "Garden of Magic" and the vocal version "Sarah's Theme." Some people simply call it "Sarah's Song."[5]

Whichever name you land on, Horner's composition — adapted by Debney in the final arrangement — is absolutely haunting in each of its iterations. Its first appearance has a lilting quality about it, as if some antique toy from the Renaissance wound itself up in your attic at around 3 a.m. and started to play. And when it transitions into the next cue, an all-female choir "ooohs" the melody like an overture to doom.

Later, when Parker sings, the instrumentation takes a different approach. Whereas the music for "I Put a Spell on You" was performed on-screen by the skeleton band, Sarah's accompaniment comes from outside the characters' world (typical of musicals). The orchestration cascades in on mallets, the notes raining from the sky but sneakily so. There is a persistent whisper in the recording — an ambient kind of white noise — with a lone, howling string singing in the distant background. Behind that, we hear chirping crickets. Here again, the score simulates the sound of wind as Winnie commands, "Use thy voice, Sarah, fill the sky!" And what a sky it is. Flying high above Salem (well, neighboring Marblehead, Massachusetts, if you want to know the truth of it), the witches bring us one of the most vivid shots in the film (see the next page). Their command of the dark horizon accentuates the palpable sense of jeopardy in the song.

Parker's voice is remarkably alluring, occasionally breaking into a whisper of its own. This is very much a siren song, only Sarah's not so much a mermaid as a pied piper on a broom. Her lyrics are suggestive, verging on seductive. And in light of her nymphomaniacal outbursts elsewhere — "Boys will love me!" and "Hang him on a hook and let me play with him," et al — it's fair to ask, what exactly *is* this "garden of magic"? (In the next chapter, we'll take a closer look at what Sarah might mean here. Hint: it's not about "children," *per se*.)

Sensuality flourishes on nights when the moon is swollen. It's impossible to divorce the music from the bewitching visuals the movie marries it to. The whole aesthetic is punch-drunk on Halloween. This is full-moon music — beaming, bulging, and worthy of a Witch City escapade on All Hallows' Eve.

Chapter Seven

The Brave Little Virgin

As the credits roll, newcomers ask one question more than any other: "Um, what's with all the virgin talk?"

Naturally, like most Disney movies, *Hocus Pocus* has its eye on sex and those who haven't had it yet. Okay, that isn't actually true of a single other Disney film, a fact that makes *Hocus Pocus* a captivating anomaly.

Virginity is central to its premise. The witches can't come back without a virgin to summon them, and it is our protagonist, Max, who arrives with the requisite chastity and bravado. He is very much a virgin, and the screenplay reminds us of this again and again and again. In fact, the movie mentions virginity approximately once every ten minutes on average. Often, those references arrive in the form of teasing, as the rest of the characters enjoy an eye roll or a laugh at Max's temperance. At other times, there is almost a reverence toward it. "Brave little virgin who lit the candle," Sarah says, "I'll be thy friend."

This is all very intriguing. "What's with all the virgin talk," indeed? Why would a PG-rated, Disney-branded musical comedy make much ado about virginity, particularly in 1993?

Surely, this didn't happen by accident. Virginity doesn't write itself onto a screenplay page. The plot point could not have been, if you'll pardon the expression, miraculously conceived. Someone put it there — over and over. Having seen a number of Disney films myself, I can assure you, while the studio is no stranger to edgy themes, it has never been in the habit of bandying casual sex talk. And yet here it is, on the lips of child actors in a family film. Why?

Given its prevalence, we can reasonably speculate virginity might be of real thematic significance to this film and its story. And if so, we can further suppose this central theme might help us understand why audiences have reacted to *Hocus Pocus* so intensely. It seems unlikely there would be no connection between a theme as powerful as virginity in a family film and the staying power this movie has enjoyed among late-Gen-X-ers and millennials. The question of virginity in the movie is ubiquitous in the blogosphere, and as we'll see toward the end of this book, it even colors the stage adaptation at Walt Disney World's Magic Kingdom. Max's virginal odyssey seems to have made quite an impact on audiences.

Scholars routinely grapple with the roles sex and virginity play in the catalogues of Alfred Hitchcock, Tim Burton, Billy Wilder, Stanley Kubrick, and many others. Indeed, wherever critics identify sex as a prominent (or even latent) theme in a film, they are called upon to examine the how and why of it. One of the central arguments of this book is that *Hocus Pocus* is as fine and worthy a film as any other commanding a rapt audience. Accordingly, its interaction with virginity ought to be considered just as seriously. And as it turns out, we find some *fascinating* insights when we start peeling back those layers.

Consider this: would we have even thought about whether the characters are virgins had the film not brought it up? Would we have simply assumed them to be virgins, given their age and that this is a Disney film? If so, why does the movie invite us to think about their sexual experience in the first place? Do we *need* to think about that to understand the movie properly? What's really going on in *Hocus Pocus*?

What Sarah's Song Really Means

So far, we've dealt with a straightforward, surface-level reading of the story, which more or less looks like this:

In the late 1600s, three sister-witches prophesy their return at the hands of a candle-lighting virgin. Fast-forward a few centuries, and fresh-from-L.A. Max Dennison shows up with a V-card in one hand and a lighter in the other. With a click of his Zippo, Max brings the witches back, and they immediately begin their quest to "suck the life out of all the children in Salem." In furtherance of that goal, Sarah Sanderson casts a siren's spell over the city: "Come, little children, I'll take thee away..." And just like that, the young masses zombie their way to the streets, marching mindlessly toward Salem's woods.

The narrative basically jells on a casual viewing, but upon closer inspection, the sisters' spell seems strangely selective. The ages of those affected versus those who are not is inconsistent. Max and Allison, for instance, do not fall under the spell, while others around their age (or older) do. And the witches are bafflingly picky about the children they'll devour. Might another reading of the film, then, make more sense?

Let's try a theory on for size. Maybe when the Sanderson sisters say they need to suck the lives out of "children," what they really mean is "virgins." In turn, perhaps the lyrics "come, little children" are actually code for "come, little virgins." And maybe Max is only a virgin for the first two acts of the film.

Now, before moving forward, I want to distinguish my inquiries here from the kind of hyper-sexed conspiracy theories we often encounter when talking about Disney films. We've all heard that the stars in the sky of *The Lion King* spell "SEX," a priest in *The Little Mermaid* reveals his manhood while wedding Prince Eric to Ursula, or the title character in *Aladdin* whispers, "Good teenagers, take off your clothes." Those theories are but baseless urban legends, and they have been thoroughly and credibly debunked.[1] Neither this book nor its author subscribes to such silliness, and that's not the kind of conjecture we're going to pursue here.

Likewise, before we tumble into Tumblr territory and start grasping for straws, let us distinguish this theory from the kind of hackneyed hypotheses that put every Pixar film in the same universe or have *Back to the Future* predicting 9/11 some sixteen years in advance.[2] Those proposals, intriguing as they might be, typically require extraordinary leaps, whereas this "come, little virgins" theory might limit our leaps instead.

In writing about sex and double entendre in *Bringing Up Baby* (a mostly wholesome comedy from 1938), film scholar Stanley Cavell cautions that, while discussing the film's sexual references is indispensable to properly understanding the film, he is reluctant to press them too far for fear of "betraying the film's subtlety of representation."[3] I'd like to borrow that caveat for *Hocus Pocus* too.

There isn't anything salacious about *Hocus Pocus*'s approach to sex or virginity, nor is it especially on the nose. I do not believe and will not argue it engages in any kind of indoctrination or scandalizing. The movie is essentially "good clean fun," as the parents of 1993 might have called it, and this book isn't here to suggest otherwise. But we can't deny that the concept of virginity is recurring throughout, or that audiences of *most* ages likely have at least a distant or hazy understanding of what that concept means.[4] It is a significant part of the film and ought to be considered as such.

Naturally, whenever we look for "more" in a movie, there's the risk that searching will leave us in the weeds. And it goes without saying none of us (your author included) can peer inside a filmmaker's mind. My argument, then, isn't so much that the *Hocus Pocus* scribes *intended* for us to read the film this way, but rather that as an audience, we are *invited* to so read. As opposed to some of those other, wackadoodle hypotheses, the evidence in support of this theory will come exclusively from the script itself, the *mise-en-scène*, and the exercise of ordinary logic — consistent with the kinds of readings regularly employed in the study of other, more "serious" films. In the end, you might find not only are some of the movie's most notorious plot holes suddenly filled but we also finally have a plausible explanation for why there's all that "virgin talk" in the first place.

Sex and the City (of Salem)

So let's look at the story again, this time in light of my proposal.

The film opens with Sarah flying by the Binx bedroom in 1693, singing her virgin-catcher of a spell. Unknowingly bewitched, young Emily follows. We meet two other youths around the same time: Emily's brother, Thackery, and his friend, Elijah. They aren't hoodwinked, so clearly these sly devils know their way around a bedroom (as if their chest-baring DiCaprio vibes weren't clues enough).

An early shot establishes Emily and Thackery as sharing a bedroom. Upon waking, Thackery is surprised she isn't there. We learn later in the film Sarah's spell can rouse children from their sleep, *including* those around Thackery's age. So it should entice him too (were it for children, literally), but it doesn't.

Thackery takes off after Emily and spies on the witches in their cottage, where we learn at least two pertinent facts: Mary can smell "children," and drinking the life force of "children" makes them younger.

Once Thackery is in the cottage, there is some confusion as to whether he's a viable target for the witches. Mary smells a child but isn't sure if it's just because Emily is there.[5] Winifred threatens to brew another batch for Thackery, but even though he's an easy target, the witches never attempt to drink his life force. They turn him into a cat instead. An experienced lad like Thackery won't make them any younger, so they look for a more torturous punishment.

Three centuries later, Max, Allison, and Dani are in the cottage by themselves. Allison tells Max a *virgin* would have to light the black-flame candle, to which Max swaggeringly replies, "So let's light the sucker."

"Will you do the honors?" he asks.

"No thanks," Allison replies, with her best "bitch, please."

I am hardly the first person to theorize Allison's demur here as evidence of her post-virginity. Vinessa Shaw has even hinted at it herself, and it's a popular point of observation online, though the authors seldom explore the idea any further.[6]

The witches return soon thereafter, and notably, they *never* directly pursue Allison. Only Max and Dani, the virgins. Their chase fuels the ensuing action throughout the second act, leading us to the pivotal scene in which, I submit, Max loses his virginity — at least metaphorically.

After burning the witches in the school furnace, our heroes return to the Dennison house to finally get some sleep. Upstairs, cuddled in low lighting, Max and Allison exchange a few romantic glances before Allison falls asleep on Max. Immediately, the camera cuts to the high school exterior, where a pillar of green smoke drives itself from the sky and back into the chimney opening. Simultaneously, we hear a high-pitched scream. Then the camera cuts to the furnace door popping open, with the witches walking out of it.

Recognizing Max's symbolic deflowering in this scene requires an understanding of how sex has traditionally been expressed in cinema when the confines of the studio or the genre didn't allow it.

Even though we usually think about "old movies" as being "clean," the truth is sex has been one of the dominant themes of American cinema nearly since its inception. But during the early Pre-Code (pre-1930) and Hays Code (1930-1968) eras, when Hollywood dealt with sex, it did so only through subtle implication and plausible deniability.[7] Audiences wouldn't have stood for brazen sexuality and, more to the point, neither would Congress.

As a matter of fact, the Hays Code existed largely as an effort to avoid

Congressional regulation of American cinema. By policing itself, Hollywood reasoned it could avoid the heavy hand of Uncle Sam in its artistic
endeavors. But Hollywood's hand turned out to be just as heavy. The Code
was *strict*, so if characters had sex, you only knew it because a bedspread
would suddenly ruffle, or because a quick cut of the camera and a steamy
glance implied intimacy.

Significantly, sex did not always transpire literally, and certainly not
on-screen. Rather, audiences were invited to understand sex had happened
despite the lack of it in any obvious way.

The great purveyors of 1960s cinema were especially clever about skirt-
ing Code rules, Hitchcock[8] and Wilder[9] chief among them. The "New
Hollywood" of the 1960s-70s was a sexier brand of cinema, the kind
moralists lamented as "anything goes."

Hitchock's *North by Northwest* (1959) lifted an early middle finger to
the Code in its final scene, wherein Roger pulls the object of his affection,
Kate, into a bed and engages her in a passionate kiss. The camera immediately and abruptly cuts to a train hurtling into a tunnel, a highly visual
but plausibly deniable implication of sex.

North by Northwest *(1959). MGM. Available from Warner Home Video.*

In *Out of the Past* (1947), the leads sit on a couch and kiss once, his lips on her neck. Mid-kiss, Robert Mitchum's character throws a towel at a nearby lamp and the camera follows it, taking the characters out of view. The lamp falls, the lights go out, and the front door suddenly swings open, revealing heavy rain and a loud clap of thunder outside.

Out of the Past *(1947). RKO Radio Pictures. Available from Warner Home Video.*

In Wilder's *Double Indemnity* (1944), Walter and Phyllis, who have fallen in love and joined in a conspiracy to kill Phyllis's husband, sit together on a sofa. It's late at night, and Phyllis has snuck over to Walter's apartment without her husband's knowledge. "We just sat there," Walter narrates, as the camera dollies back and the scene dissolves away. By assuring us they didn't have sex, Walter invites us to consider maybe they have. Minutes later, we return to the apartment to find Walter reclined and smoking a cigarette while Phyllis reapplies her makeup in a mirror. Critics have joined in a consensus that the characters sleep together in the scene (or at least they *probably* do, as Roger Ebert supposed), even though it certainly doesn't happen in any literal way. "In 1944 movies you can't be sure," Ebert said.[10]

Top: Double Indemnity *(1944). Paramount. Available from Universal Home Entertainment.*

We might find this same kind of play at work in *Hocus Pocus*. Max and Allison's nuzzling is as innocent as anything we see on-screen from the '40s, '50s, or '60s, but the abrupt cut from their cuddle to the green smoke

entering the chimney immediately calls Hitchcock's train tunnel to mind. The loud feminine scream from the still-dead Winifred and the swinging furnace door — not unlike the front door in *Out of the Past* — might imply sex, as might the metaphor of birth when the witches walk out of the oven, reborn. When we return to Max and Allison, we see Winifred's book open its eye, a familiar metaphor for new knowledge. Allison arises, exchanges a knowing half-smile with Max, and then expresses alarm over how much time has passed.

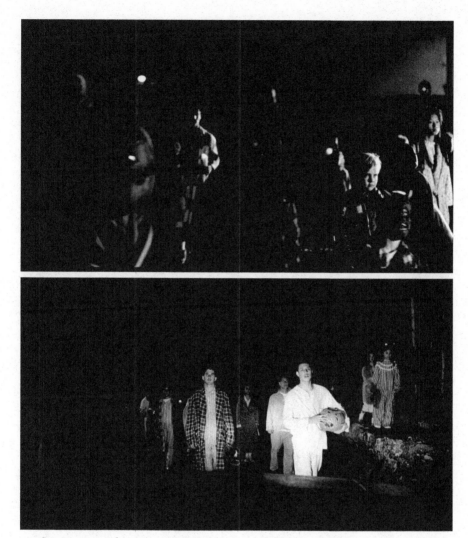

On its own, the green smoke scene would be suggestive, certainly, but perhaps insufficient to support a reading of Max's lost virginity without any additional support from the narrative. But the story from this point won't make much sense *unless* we believe Max is no longer a virgin. (Notably, while he has asserted his virginity several times in the film up to this point, you won't hear him say it again after this scene.)

When Sarah sings her song the second time, flying high over 1993 Salem at night, she brings a whole horde of youth to the streets, spellbound.

In the foreground, we find mostly very young children. But a closer look reveals something very interesting about the "children" marching behind them. Many of them are older — at least as old as Max and Allison, if not collegiate, their age made no secret thanks to unbuttoned men's pajama tops revealing clearly muscular physiques. These are not children in the literal sense, which leaves us to figure out *why* they're under Sarah's spell. Max and Allison certainly aren't spellbound, so if "child" refers to age, these scenes make no sense. But if "child" refers to virginal status, the delineation becomes clearer. Max and Allison look down on the marching virgins from Max's bedroom high above, its elevation symbolic of the gulf of life experience that now separates them. Max has "overcome" his virginity and, no longer a child himself, must now save his little sister.

Sure enough, he *does* save her — but how? As we arrive at the film's final scenes, we stumble on another would-be plot hole remedied by our new understanding of Max as post-virginal.

A regular Katniss Everdeen, Max swipes Winifred's potion in the graveyard and downs the bottle himself, making it virtually impossible for the witches to consume Dani before daybreak. Though she'd set her heart on exacting personal revenge against the littlest Dennison, Winifred reluctantly agrees to feast on Max's soul instead. She gets a few good-sized gulps down as the sun starts to peek over the horizon, but nothing changes. Her hair turns no redder, her face no fuller. She sucks some more. Still nothing. Not a day of added youth. And the gulping continues. Compared to the relatively tiny sips the Sandersons took from Emily earlier in the film, this is a smorgasbord, a soul-swallowing suckfest. So why doesn't it work?

Clearly, Winifred has no qualms with Max's age. There's no sense of "Oh, great, a *teenager* drank my potion, so I'm out of luck." Let's ask ourselves, then, what does Winifred know about Max, aside from his age?

Remember: he's the one who lit the black-flame candle. So she knows he is a virgin. But what she doesn't know, aside from the logistics of Daylight Saving Time, is while she and her sisters were crying in their cottage, Max lost his V-card. And *that's* why the potion doesn't work.[11]

On the one hand, none of this should come as a tremendous surprise. It is a common trope of film and literature that witches, monsters, and other villains must consume the life force of a virgin to become younger, stronger, or immortal. Likewise, in another common trope, whenever film characters establish their virginities in a story, those virginities are often "resolved" by the film's end. We see both these tropes at work in our reading of *Hocus Pocus*. Moreover, scholars have noted a longstanding association between virginity and sacrificial victims in horror.[12] (The next chapter will look more closely at this theme in the context of horror.)

On the other hand, there *is* something surprising about finding sacrificial virgins in a 1993 Disney film. Mind you, sex isn't altogether
absent in the Disney pantheon. It is clearly implied in *The Lion King*
(Simba and Nala romp in the jungle; shortly thereafter, a cub is born),
Lady and the Tramp (the eponymous dogs curl up on a hill; fade to black,
and Lady is pregnant), and *101 Dalmatians* ("Where did they all come
from?" Anita asks of the new puppies, to which Roger replies, "Pongo,
you old rascal!"), among many other others, but almost always in the
context of procreation.

Hocus Pocus engages with sex on a different level. I imagine those
who will deem my theory too big a pill to swallow might accuse me of
"reading sex into a Disney film" (a trend I generally deplore), but I would
remind them sex was very much a part of this movie before I ever saw it.
Max's virginity is a crucial plot point, and by repeatedly referencing it,
the film extends an invitation for us to read it with that in mind.

It might be fair to ask, if the movie needs us to know Max has sex,
why not come right out and say it? The world was progressive enough in
1993, right? In the 1930s – 1960s, it was the Hays Code and the mores
of the day that kept sex subtle. But the Code crumbled decades before
Hocus Pocus came around. The MPAA stands in its place today, a more
permissive (and still privately regulated) agency, responsible for our G,
PG, PG-13, R, and NC-17.

But isn't it possible to think about the Disney brand as a "Hays Code"
all its own? A certain set of standards, expectations, and ethics attach to
that brand, and those expectations are nearly universally understood.
This is the studio, after all, that in 1993 (the same year as *Hocus Pocus*)
refused to brand *The Nightmare Before Christmas* a Disney film for fear
it was too dark, too edgy. The confines a Disney filmmaker might face
aren't altogether different from those Hitchock or Wilder faced under
the Code.

So if you had a family-adventure story to tell in 1993 and sex/vir-
ginity played a part, but you were releasing it under the Disney banner,
mightn't you need to approach those topics with the same delicate song
and dance that filmmakers of a bygone era employed?

Whether that was the intention or not, the supposedly "silly" *Hocus Pocus* might actually make more sense when we approach it like the Hitchcockian masterpieces it mirrors, treating it to the serious film study it deserves.

Chapter Eight

Is *Hocus Pocus* a Horror Film?

One of my favorite Halloween traditions is the movie marathon. Each fall, I host a two-night, eight-movies film fest, complete with autumnal snacks and desserts themed to match. Marshmallow "teeth" are haphazardly glued (with peanut butter) to apple-slice "mouths" in honor of Steve Martin's dentist in *Little Shop of Horrors*. Unsettling chunks of I'm-not-sure-what get baked into "Mrs. Lovett's Meat Pies" for *Sweeney Todd*. Chocolate chips turn bananas into "boo-nanas" for *Ghostbusters*. And whatever's on the screen, there's always a pumpkin sliced in half and filled with ice, the ultimate bottle-cooler centerpiece — sometimes with the "slasher's knife" still jutting out the side.

The parties have grown more elaborate over the years, and these days, every attendee gets a vote in choosing which movies make the cut. To accommodate divergent tastes, there are now two ballots: "Horror" (*Halloween*, *The Exorcist*, *The Shining*, et al.) and "Festive/Family" (*Beetlejuice*, *E.T.*, *Halloweentown*, etc.). Unfailingly, *Hocus Pocus* has appeared on the latter... we figure it's more festive than frightening. But maybe we've been wrong about that.

Horror is not an easy thing to define. In terms of movies, it's meant ghosts, gore, violence, magic, monsters, minor chords, suspense, and sur-prise — but the absence of any one of those doesn't preclude a film from getting classified as horror. So how are we supposed to draw the line between horror and everything else? Maybe it's best to borrow Supreme Court Justice Potter Stewart's definition for obscenity: we know it when we see it. Do we, though?

The question of whether *Hocus Pocus* is really a "horror" film arises repeatedly on the web. I imagine, for many readers, the answer is an obvious "no." *Saw* this is not, nor is it *Paranormal Activity*. But what makes those movies horror and something like *Hocus Pocus* different?

Defining horror becomes most interesting when we consider movies that don't cleanly fit the easiest rubric but for which we can nevertheless make a case, movies like *The Silence of the Lambs*, *The Wicker Man*, *Alien*, *The Manchurian Candidate*, *Jurassic Park*, *Jaws*, *Gravity*, or *Ghost*. Let's add *Hocus Pocus* to that list while we're at it.

Understanding the horror genre is important because it is fundamen-tally about that which scares or disgusts us, and so it provides an invaluable tool for working through those things. It also helps us understand what societies fear on a more global scale, particularly whenever an audience has demonstrated a strong emotional response to a given horror work. In what critics call a "symptomatic reading," we can look back at a movie and "diagnose" the underlying anxieties of the culture in which that film was made and embraced. The threats in the movie often mirror the perceived threats of its time, even if they only become clear in retrospect. (Inciden-tally, this is often true of villains in superhero films too.)

A lot has been written about horror, and absolutely no one — not even the experts or insiders — can agree on a litmus test. In surveying the literature on the topic, though, we *can* find at least six traits on which there is some consensus:

The Archetypes of Horror: The scoffing authority figure, the wise elder who recognizes the evil, the screaming victim, the prolonged minor chord. The tropes of horror are well worn but irresistible nonetheless. The setting and mood are foreboding, owing to the genre's literary roots... gothic mansions, castles, abbeys, haunted houses, graveyards, and the like.

And at some point, we will usually see our heroes react to something in a display of visceral repulsion or physical disgust.[1] You won't find every staple in every film, but if it's horror, at least a few are bound to turn up.

An Impossible Threat: The villains or threats in horror (critics refer to them collectively as "the monster") are usually supernatural in nature, irrational or impossible in the real world. The threats tend to originate in some distant past or in a poorly understood series of events, later pieced together from remnants discovered by our protagonists. And no matter who's playing the hero, it's usually the *monster* that audiences come to see.[2]

Teenage Prey: At least since the 1970s, horror's heroes (and victims) tend to be teenagers, especially in slasher films, though there are plenty of exceptions.[3]

The Theme of Isolation: Our protagonists are often on their own — different than, or separate from, everyone else.[4]

Social Repression: Horror films have a tendency to impart social lessons, especially morals tied into some religious value. The basic narrative formula is one in which normality (that is, a dominant social norm) is threatened by the monster. The monster is essentially a shadow of normality — Mr. Hyde is a shadow of Dr. Jekyll, for example, and Dr. Frankenstein's creation of the monster mirrors his own marital engagement. This is called "The Doppelganger Motif." In this way, the central conflict typically deals with something repressed in society — usually sexual repression, or perhaps an "Other" who has been socially oppressed.[5]

The Fear Response: Simply put, horror films scare us.

⤬

Let's explore *Hocus Pocus* with this "horror flick checklist" in mind.

The Archetypes of Horror

From an abandoned cottage-turned-museum in the woods (essentially a haunted house) to an enlivened graveyard, *Hocus Pocus* puts us in the middle of a gothic wonderland. I wouldn't be surprised if the movie's nods

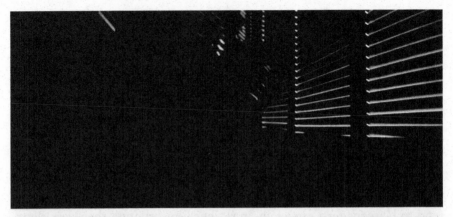

Top: Halloween *(1978). Compass International Pictures; Falcon International Productions. Available from Ancbor Bay Entertainment.*

to classical horror are part of what pulls people in. Even if we aren't ready to call it "horror" just yet, it certainly borrows liberally from films that decidedly are. There are plenty of screams (Dani's got lungs!) and scoffing authority figures, from the incredulous skeleton band to the virgin-taunting wannabe cop, and Dani is visibly disgusted when she meets Billy the zombie. Debney's score repeatedly employs prolonged, dissonant minor chords to evoke suspense, and the camera adopts handheld rhythms and unsettling vantage points whenever it wants us to feel on edge. Most notable is the shot from inside Max's closet, the camera peering through the slats like a predator's peepers, immediately calling to mind Laurie's closet encounter with Michael Myers in *Halloween*.

The threat in the closet is a false alarm the first time we see it, a misdirect that turns out to be Dani spying on her brother. Later, though, in a scene filled with suspense and horror homage shots, the closet will house a real threat: Winifred and Mary, hiding inside with their demonic book.

And like the best horror villains, Winifred is hard to kill. She's hanged, incinerated, and dropped from the sky to toxic holy ground, but she always gets back up — until the end.

An Impossible Threat

The monster's impossible otherworldliness is often said to be *the* defining distinction between horror movie monsters and scary villains in other genres. Does that really hold up, though? There is nothing supernatural about Norman Bates. Is *Psycho* not horror, then? Likewise, Frankenstein's monster is more a product of technology than of magic or godliness, and the same can be said for Mr. Hyde. Sure enough, you'll find critics arguing all three of those works fall outside of horror on that basis, but a definition excluding titles most people consider emblematic of the genre is probably

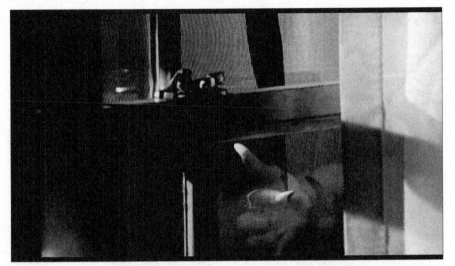

The witches invade the Dennison house in horror-like fashion.

a definition in need of revision.

At any rate, the Sanderson sisters are undeniably supernatural, incompatible with the real world. Then again, so are most of the bad guys in Disney films. What about Maleficent, Ursula, and Jafar? If *Aladdin* is a horror movie, we've probably gone too far.

Noël Carroll wrote one of the earliest and most important books on horror cinema, tackling this problem head-on:

> "What appears to demarcate the horror story from mere stories with monsters, such as myths [or fairy tales], is the attitude of characters in the story to the monsters they encounter. In works of horror, the humans regard the monsters they meet as abnormal, as disturbances of the natural order. In fairy tales, on the other hand, monsters are part of the everyday furniture of the universe... A creature like Chewbacca in the space opera *Star Wars* is just one of the guys, though a creature gotten up in the same wolf outfit, in a film like *The Howling*, would be regarded with utter revulsion by the human characters in that fiction."[6]

Carroll's definition distinguishes the witches in *Hocus Pocus* from witches in *Sleeping Beauty* or *The Wizard of Oz*. The Wicked Witch of the West is a threat to Dorothy and frightens her (and even us), but she is not a disturbance of the natural order because witches and magic are not foreign to the world of Oz. In contrast, the Sandersons are fish out of water.

Another critic, Rick Worland, is more cautious about drawing a rigid line between the genres, especially when it comes to horror, fantasy, and sci-fi. But he does identify a distinction: in horror, magic is wrapped up in the black arts, the occult, or death. Fantasy, meanwhile, is about non-occult magic, and sci-fi is about the supremacy of human's efforts in research and technology over *any* supernatural force.[7]

Interestingly, while *Hocus Pocus* probably straddles Worland's horror/fantasy divide, the screenplay goes to great lengths to connect its magic directly with the occult. The witches talk at length about their passion for Hell, the time they've spent there, and their loyalty to Satan. Their spells are ritualistic and sacrificial.[8] We're told Winifred's spell book is bound in human flesh, a gift from the devil himself. It's all a tad tongue-in-cheek, but at the same time, this is astoundingly stark stuff for a contemporary Disney film.

Teenage Prey

Clearly, all three of our heroes are teenagers (Max and Allison) or preteens (Dani). Thackery, though trapped in a cat's body for 300 years, is an imprisoned teenage soul too. The witches spend most of the movie stalking them, so it looks like we have a third box to check here. But even if *Hocus Pocus* is ultimately a horror film, it is also a family film — and teenagers are common protagonists in both genres. So let's not make too much of that.

Whenever teenagers are victims in horror movies, especially slasher films, their deaths are usually connected directly to their sexuality. In *Halloween*, the seminal slasher flick, teens tend to die shortly after having sex on-screen. It is only Laurie, our virginal protagonist, who survives 'til the end.

Laurie is the quintessential "Final Girl," a term film critics use to describe the teenage woman — almost always a virgin — who is stalked by the slasher in such films.[9] She is the primary protagonist and, ultimately, a survivor. The implication is she survives *because* of her virginity. Purity, like courage, is a virtue. Her slasher, conversely, is almost always male, and usually a repressed virgin himself.

Given that a teenage virgin figures so prominently in *Hocus Pocus*, it's interesting to think about the extent to which Max might be a "Final Girl." He is male, of course, but his hunter (Winifred) is female, and that would make *Hocus Pocus* a fascinating inversion of the typical Final Girl narrative.[10] Thackery echoes the inversion when he refers to Max as "some airhead virgin," "airhead" having historically been a gendered pejorative associated with "dumb blondes."[11]

The Theme of Isolation

Max feels lonely because he's in a new place without any friends to call his own. Remember: the Dennisons have just moved to Salem from LA. Donning a tie-dye shirt and doodling The Grateful Dead in his notebook, Max is ridiculed by his classmates, rejected (at first) by the girl he likes, and harassed by bullies who steal his candy and his shoes. He storms into his house and shouts about how much he hates it here in Salem, and he later confesses his loneliness to Dani while the two recline on a bale of hay. He feels isolated in a strange place, a feeling that turns up in so many horror movies, in part because it helps to ease the audience into a feeling of foreboding or danger.[12]

Social Repression

Most horror movies are fundamentally "about" something. *Halloween* is about chastity and moral decline in contemporary America (a so-called "slut slasher"). *Psycho* is about the vulnerabilities of suburban life, the weight of guilt, and the mother-son relationship (Marion Crane is killed while doing the most normal thing imaginable, taking a shower, but she's in the motel in the first place because she's hiding a secret... and her killer is a smothered "mother's boy"). These are but two examples among many horror films that connect their monsters with some sort of suppressed human instinct or unspoken social struggle.

If *Hocus Pocus* is "about" something other than trick-or-treating and some campy laughs, it is surely about the pressure on Max to have sex, something we've already explored at length in the previous chapter. It's intriguing, though, to think about the way sexuality is represented in *Hocus Pocus*, and how it turns up in other horror films.

Influential (and radical) film theorist Robin Wood argued horror movies should be interpreted like dreams. He noted our tendency to watch scary movies in the dark, often with the stated goal of "losing ourselves" in the fantasy and the horror — an escape from wakefulness, from reality, into a type of sleep.

Sigmund Freud suggested our dreams are visually symbolic methods of self-communication, a way for us to hash out emotional conflict and trauma. Our fears and desires emerge, but only behind a mask. Wood and many other critics look at horror movies the same way, assuming many of the figures and encounters in the movies are symbols, society's hidden fears and desires in thin disguise.[13]

"Yabbos" are an especially interesting symbol in *Hocus Pocus*. That's Max's word for breasts, as Dani painfully points out in front of Allison — a mortifying exchange that undoubtedly cast a cringe over an entire generation. (To this day, it's one of the most quoted lines in the movie). Later, Max's own mother calls attention to her breasts, accentuated in an iconic Madonna cone costume.[14] Later still, Sarah's cleavage is made prominent and central to the frame during her broom ride over Salem.

Fixation on the female anatomy is hardly uncommon in Hollywood, but in a film where the main character is taunted for sexual inexperience, the repeated allusion to breasts is significant, especially given that this is a family film. It might be that these references underscore Max's feeling that sex (and the pressure to have sex) is all around him, everywhere he looks. Perhaps it's no coincidence Sarah is so fond of saying, "Amok! Amok! Amok!" In common parlance, the word's most frequent usage is in reference to "a world run amok" with sin.

Many bloggers have asked whether *Hocus Pocus* "shames" virgins, given how much Max is mocked. If so, that would be fairly revolutionary. For

all its hypersexuality, Hollywood's core message in movies about teenage sex and virginity has been to reinforce dominant sexual norms. In other words, as we saw with *Halloween*, even if a horror movie delights in sex and nudity for ninety minutes, the purest character ultimately wins out. But that kind of reading gets complicated in *Hocus Pocus*, if we accept Max as no longer a virgin at the end.

Let's look at things from Max's perspective. How confusing — terri- fying, even — must the world feel when, amidst all your teenage angst, the people in your new town hound you to lose your virginity? Teens in horror films are "clearly confused and overwhelmed by sex,"[15] even when it is all around them.

We might read the film, then, as a dreamlike representation of the teenage male's experience in 1993 America — pressured to shed innocence in a sexually enlightened yet culturally conservative society. The movie doesn't "virgin shame," then, so much as it comments *on* virgin shaming. The horror Max faces is simply the pressure to grow up, to come of age. If this is a horror movie, it is Max's own virginity that haunts him.

The Fear Response

The final item on our "horror checklist" is the most difficult for any fan who wants to call *Hocus Pocus* a horror movie. Is it really all that scary?

One of the perennial guests at my Halloween movie marathons grumbles whenever *Hocus Pocus* makes the cut because, as a serious horror fan, he's annoyed that the witches are more comical than malevolent. Undoubtedly, no adult is losing sleep at night after even a first-time viewing of *Hocus Pocus*. But those of us who were lucky enough to meet the movie as kids might have memories of genuine fear while watching (and for some time thereafter).

In his book *Projected Fears*, a study of popular horror films, Kendall R. Phillips polls people about their favorite scary movies and describes their responses:

> "While many are traditional horror films, it's surprising how often films from other genres appear, including the remarkably pervasive fear evoked by *The Wizard of Oz*... Horror films, perhaps more than any other type of film, seem to impact people's lives. In fairness, the biggest impression is often when we are children or adolescents and are beginning to struggle with the societal boundaries and forbidden knowledge... Each of us experiences film individually, and our different tastes in films demonstrate

how unique our individual reactions are. Yet, what are we to make of those films that seem to have tapped into the collective fears of an entire generation? Can we have what film theorist Robin Wood calls, 'collective nightmares'? If so, how should we seek to understand those 'projected nightmares' that seem to affect our broader culture?"[16]

Even if *Hocus Pocus* isn't terrifying, it just might qualify as one of those "collective nightmares," like *The Wizard of Oz*. Besides, *Frankenstein* never kept me up at night either. [17]

Ortega effectively captures the film's prevailing tone in this arresting shot. It is scary and intense (especially for young viewers), but at the same time, there is a playful campiness about it. The frame would work as a horror poster or as a girl group's album cover.

I don't know that the world will ever quite agree on exactly what constitutes "horror." As long as there are people who say *Frankenstein* isn't but *Jaws* is, there's room for debate. Heck, there is a whole camp out there that insists *It's a Wonderful Life* is essentially a horror film.

Even if you think the question of whether *Hocus Pocus* is horror is ridiculous, surely it is *less* ridiculous than asking whether it is science fiction, a crime drama, or a western. If nothing else, the movie helps itself to the conventions of horror in a way that makes it not quite like the comedy-fantasies we've come to expect from Disney.[18] The movie flirts with fear, and it's got more game than Max when he tries to ask out Allison with that awful Jimi Hendrix line (the other cringe heard 'round the world).

This dance with the devil might be why whole generations find the film so provocative and exciting. To borrow a phrase from Phillips, it teases us (at least as children) with "forbidden knowledge."

Come this Halloween, I doubt I'll take *Hocus Pocus* off the "Festive/Family" ballot at my movie marathon, but maybe this time it'll have an asterisk and the world's longest footnote at the end.

Chapter Nine

Of All the Witches Working:

Feminism in Disney's Villainesses

W inifred Sanderson is evil and loving it. Ask her sisters; she's *vicious* — and proud. "Of all the witches working," she blusters with Trump-ish aplomb, "I'm the worst." Is she, though? Out of *all* the witches? Because that's *quite* a coven, even if only Disney witches were on the guest list.

The Sanderson sisters are a distinctly 1990s brand of Disney witch, though the decade saw fewer Disney witches than most. Naturally, whenever Hollywood puts a witch on camera, questions arise about that character as a representation of women in society. Feminists and scholars have wrangled with whether to see Hollywood's witches as heroines for feminism or as the scapegoats of a sexist hegemony. On the one hand, these are women who are literally empowered. On the other, they're typically cast as ugly, evil outsiders who must ultimately perish for being powerful.

Hocus Pocus serves something for both camps to chew on. The Sanderson sisters aren't the mirror-on-the-wall witches of yore, nor are they *quite* feminist exemplars. But it is possible, I think, to read the female characters in this film as progressive and, in many ways, even feminist.

Academics are interested in Disney's female characters because of their large audience, their popularity among impressionable children, and their long-lasting appeal. As Professor Amy M. Davis writes, "In their representations of femininity, Disney films reflected the attitudes of the wider society from which they emerged... their enduring popularity is evidence that the depictions they contain would continue to resonate as the films were re-released in later decades."[1]

Davis is the author of *Good Girls & Wicked Witches: Women in Disney's Feature Animation*, a well-researched text that challenges the conventional wisdom in which Disney films teach young girls to be passive participants in their own lives or to define their lives in terms of a man. Davis doesn't argue there isn't any truth to that notion, but rather that the issue is simply much more complex. The broad-brush attack on Disney is based, she argues, on just two movies: *Snow White and the Seven Dwarfs* and *Cinderella*. (I might add *Sleeping Beauty* to that list.) However wonderful and redeeming those films may be in so many other respects, their eponymous heroines demonstrate relatively little agency of their own. There are *many* Disney movies, though, and as Davis traces with a careful eye, the studio's animated canon is more a "mixed bag" of feminism than an all-out assault on impressionable female minds. Stated differently, the truth of a matter is almost always more sophisticated than a blanket statement would imply.

Feminist film analysis often focuses on a handful of key metrics: the character's motivations, her appearance, her sexuality, her relationship with the movie's men, her relationship with the other women, her actions (and the extent to which those actions exhibit agency), whether the plot would still work without her, and what ultimately happens to her in the end. In tandem, those considerations guide us toward a critical understanding of that character's role in the movie and the way in which she represents the role of womanhood in the world.

Davis uses that type of framework to look at the evolving nature of women in Disney animation over the years, and her observations about witches in particular are useful for us here. In the studio's early days, Disney witches were strong, powerful, and bold agents of their own lives

— but also ugly, motivated by an insane jealousy, older than the youthful protagonists they opposed, and ultimately destroyed because of their proactivity or power. She writes:

> "The theme of these wicked women and their fates is not only that evil never goes unpunished but also that it is the evil women — the bitches — who are the strong, active, no-nonsense people who stop at nothing to get things done... real happiness seems to be linked to one trait alone — passivity. If you are willing to wait patiently for your happiness, it will surely come to you. Try to make it happen for yourself, and you will only end up defeated and alone."[2]

But the emergence of feminism as a mainstream movement during the 1960s and '70s finally started taking root in Hollywood by the '80s. When the Disney animated fairy tale began its resurgence with *The Little Mermaid* in 1989, the representation of women took a new mold. "The idea of a fairy tale princess sauntering up to her intended, preening, hips swaying, and flirting, is impossible to imagine in the earlier Disney films," Davis writes.[3] While Ariel herself is somewhat coy, she does introduce a conception of the Disney heroine that would grow increasingly self-possessed and liberated over the years to come. But Ursula, the evil squid witch who seeks to ensnare an unwitting Ariel in her premeditating tentacles, has much in common with the early Disney witches. She is evil, an Other, insanely power hungry, and if not ugly, certainly fat. And in an effort to get what she wants, she disguises herself as a conventional beauty.[4]

Unless we count the briefly seen witch at the beginning of *Beauty and the Beast* (1991) or peripheral townsfolk in *The Nightmare Before Christmas* (1993), the Sanderson sisters are the first Disney witches since Ursula, and the first and only of the 1990s. (Glenn Close's Cruella DeVil is arguably witchlike in 1996 but a non-witch nonetheless.)[5] As such, they are simultaneously defined by both the long-standing conventions of Disney witchdom[6] and "arguably the most pervasive discursive influence of the 1990s": political correctness.[7]

When the witches return from the dead a second time, they take to the streets of Salem after the trick-or-treating has come to an end. Trying to find children, Mary sniffs her way to Ice's foot, a setup for one of the movie's biggest laughs: "Yo, witch, get your face off my shoe."

Already, Ice's sexist, politically incorrect attitude is grating. But then Jay follows with, "Ah, man, how come it's always the ugly chicks that stay out late?" The Sandersons stop in their tracks and turn back toward them menacingly: "Chicks?"

It's the same hyper-awareness of language and machismo that leads Jessie Spano of "Saved by the Bell" to call out every sexist pig in Bayside High, *Jurassic Park*'s Dr. Ellie Sattler to put Dr. Hammond on blast with "We can discuss sexism in survival situations when I get back," and *Batman Returns*'s Selina Kyle to proudly proclaim, "I am Catwoman. Hear me roar." The blockbuster films and mainstream television of the late 1980s and '90s are replete with women who are very cognizant of and oppositional to sexism, even if their characters ultimately (and unwittingly) feed into problematic plot patterns despite them.

Incidentally, Davis references *Hocus Pocus* in her study of Disney, one of the few scholars to do so. She cites it as an example of a subgenre that became popular during the same period: the female buddy film, and more particularly, the witch buddy film. Other examples include *The Craft* (1996), *Practical Magic* (1998), and even TV series such as Sabrina, The Teenage Witch" (1996) and "Charmed" (1998).[8]

For Davis, it seems, the witch buddy subgenre matters because it expands the agency and antihero-dom of witches. But there might be a more important point here where *Hocus Pocus* is concerned, at least in that the movie directly counters the widely perpetuated myth that "women aren't funny."[9] On the contrary, *Hocus Pocus* is hilarious, and it is largely the female stars who make it so, their deliveries mining even more from the male-authored script than perhaps was there on the page.

It also passes the famous Bechdel test, which asks three questions of a movie: (1) Are there are least two female characters? (2) Do they talk to each other? (3) Is the conversation about something other than a man?[10]

In fact, women comprise the majority of the characters and deliver the bulk of the dialogue. In total, five of the seven leads (Winifred, Sarah, Mary, Allison, and Dani) are female. And among the human protagonists, women outnumber men two to one.

In an earlier chapter, we considered that *Hocus Pocus* inverts the female virgin/male stalker paradigm. Notably, a "female witch vs. male protagonist" conflict wouldn't turn up in Disney animation until *The Emperor's New Groove* in 2000.[11]

The movie also subverts, to at least some modest extent, a familiar narrative in which witches are decrepit old "hags" and goodness means beauty while badness means being ugly. The Sandersons are elderly in the prologue, but they spend the majority of the film as youthful women, and Sarah in particular is presented as sexy, vivacious, and beautiful. Parker was 28 at the time.

Dani even calls attention to the subversion: "It doesn't matter how young or old you are," she says, "You sold your soul! You're the ugliest thing that's ever lived, and you know it!"[12]

Of course, in highlighting that exchange, we must also concede that the insult bothers Winifred quite a bit here (whereas "chicks" seemed to offend her more than "ugly" earlier). "You die first," she tells Dani.

What are we to make of the Sanderson sisters' motivations from a feminist perspective? They are after beauty, youth, and revenge. Those are potentially problematic motives for women in film, but at the same time, it might be fair to consider that the sisters' desire for youth and vitality is more practical and less crazed than, say, the Evil Queen's quest for unsurpassed beauty in *Snow White*. The Sandersons are serious Satanists. They worship the devil *for real*. Winifred found her time in Hell "lovely." While a more contemporary and progressive screenplay might have shaded in their motivations, it's clear they aren't after good looks for their egos' sakes alone. Rather, these witches are out to further their master's agenda, whatever that may be, and so there is at least some utility to their motive.

Their quest for beauty isn't easy. Becoming young and gorgeous is hard work — they'll have to plot, scheme, and kill to get it. Davis says this is typical of witches in fantasy — a reflection of the difficulty women experience in real life, attempting to achieve unattainable societal standards of physical perfection. Here again, there are at least two ways to look at that: is the sisters' toil a feminist commentary on the unfairness and impossibility of those standards? Or does it reinforce a sexist worldview in which women are fools for trying to meet the standard in the first place but also disappointments for failing?

Until now, our discussion has focused entirely on the three Sandersons. But there is a fourth witch in this film: Dani. She doesn't have magical power, but I think it not insignificant that she spends the entirety of the film dressed as a witch. In a sense, she is a "good witch," the Glinda of Salem.[13] She might even have been the movie's most salient witch for the children of 1993, given their proximity in age. Dani is clever, independent, and self-assured, even if she does ultimately look to her older brother for protection and rescue, arguably more because he is an older relative than because he is male.[14]

Meanwhile, the writers and Vinessa Shaw each bring a real sense of agency and wherewithal to the character of Allison.[15] It is Allison — not Max — who takes us to the cottage. She is the one who discovers that salt will protect her friends and who figures out the witches will turn to dust at daybreak. It is Allison's idea to burn the witches and, perhaps most significantly, it is Allison and Dani who push the furnace door shut on the Sandersons. Max isn't even in the room. And though she isn't wearing a pointy hat, Winifred calls Allison "a clever little white witch" too.

At the end (er— beginning) of the day, the good guys vanquish the villains. As Davis would surely point out, even if the Sandersons do exhibit agency and liberation, they pay the ultimate price for it when all is said and done. But unlike so many witches in Hollywood's past, they die at the hands of non-passive protagonists, both female and male.

But it is neither the witches' death nor the heroes' resolution the movie chooses to end with. Rather, the closing shot is on two "male oppressors" who certainly do *not* win: Jay and Ice, left to row their boats 'til death, or at least until police scout the cottage or the Sandersons return again... whichever comes first.

More than anything, I am interested in the idea that in *Hocus Pocus*, we have a perfectly serviceable text for deep feminist readings from different points of view. There is *so much* at work in this film: sex, virginity, femininity, gender reversals, camp, and so on. Why isn't it being studied? Why has it been so consistently swept under the rug by the "serious" types, even as society stands up every Halloween and says, "Hey! There's something to this!" Is there something sexist about *that*?

If this weren't a quasi-musical (musicals have historically been dismissed as trivial, i.e. womanly) in which the overwhelming majority of the central characters are female, would it have been so quickly brushed aside? Must an empowered female film perish like the empowered witches of so many films before them?[16]

The movie's position in Disney history reminds me of an exchange early in its script:

> **Mary**: "We're young!"
> **Winifred**: "Well, young*er*".

We might say the same of *Hocus Pocus* as a feminist witch text. "We're progressive! ...Well, progressive-*er*." But as Winifred says, "It's a start!"

Chapter Ten

Flora, Fauna, and Merryweather

Merryweather: Oooo, I'd like to turn her into a fat old hoptoad.
Fauna: Now, dear, that isn't a very nice thing to say.
Flora: Besides, we can't. You know our magic doesn't work that way.
Fauna: It can only do good, dear, to bring joy and happiness.
Merryweather: Well, *that* would make *me* happy.

While we're on the topic of funny women in threes, let's pause to appreciate the banter, sass, and *shade* of Disney's original supernatural-sister triumvirate: Flora, Fauna, and Merryweather in *Sleeping Beauty* (1959).[1]

If anyone can give Winifred a run for her money in the "worst witch" department, it's Maleficent, widely considered Disney's greatest villain. (Technically, she's an evil fairy; I digress.) But when Maleficent drops in unannounced and says, "I really felt quite distressed at not receiving an invitation," it's Merryweather who looks her right in the eye and says, "You weren't wanted." Let me put some burning rain of death on that burn.

From left to right: Flora, Fauna, and Merryweather from Disney's Sleeping Beauty *(1959). Quintessential "Weird Sisters," they wear their personalities on their faces, three sides of the same coin.*

The Sanderson sisters bear a striking, if inexact, resemblance to the three Good Fairies of *Sleeping Beauty*, even as the two trios stand on opposite sides of the good/evil divide. The latter come to bless children, the former to curse them. But in their countenance, personalities, and ribbing repartee, they echo each other. And as women in societies of old, they play similar roles within their respective worlds.

If we were to draw direct lines between them (ignoring the colors of their dresses), Sarah's flighty, nymph-like personality most closely resembles absentminded, ices-a-cake-before-she-bakes-it Fauna — Sarah stashes rattails and dances idiotically while Fauna folds un-cracked eggs into her batter. Winifred and Flora are the heads of household: strong, decisive, insistent on calling the shots, and eager to criticize. Mary and Merryweather, meanwhile, share not only a name but also dark hair, a round face, and a readiness to diss their sisters with church-lady cheeriness (though Mary reserves her guff for Sarah, lauding Winnie with praise, while Merryweather is equally spicy toward both her sisters).[2]

> **Fauna:** I'm going to bake...
> **Flora:** And I'm making the dress...
> **Merryweather:** But you can't sew, and she's never cooked...

❦

Merryweather (modeling the dress): It looks awful.
Flora: That's because it's on you, dear.

∽≈≎

Thackery: You hag! There are not enough children in the
world to make thee young and beautiful.
Winifred: *Hag*? ...Sisters, did you *hear* what he called you?

Both sets of siblings conform to a familiar trope in popular culture:
"The Weird Sisters": a threesome of supernatural women who appear at
times of great importance in the other characters' lives. The best-known
Weird Sisters are the three witches in Shakespeare's *Macbeth*, and while
the idea didn't originate with the Bard, he is largely responsible for making
it a convention.

"I AM calm!"

Studies of the *Macbeth* witches frequently point to Flora, Fauna, and Merryweather as their conspicuous descendants. So too the Sandersons, but they better typify a closely related subtrope, "The Hecate Sisters" — Weirds who fall into three specific character types: the maiden (ditzy, blonde, and beautiful), the matron (eccentric and plump), and the crone (bitter, sharp-tongued, and smart). The Hecates are said to correspond with Freud's Id, Ego, and Superego, respectively.

The fact that they are sisters is significant beause the Weirds/Hecates are thought to be three sides of the same woman, so they bicker with one another in the way siblings do.[3]

The tropes are evidence of how readily we associate witchdom with sisterhood. In turn, that connotation lends itself to *Hocus Pocus's* story of sibling rivalry and reconciliation, which plays out so powerfully in the context of witchhood.

It is the story of three sets of siblings: Emily and Thackery, Dani and Max, and the Sandersons. More to the point, it is the story of three sisters who drive wedges between sisters and their brothers. The witches snatch Emily from Thackery and kill her in front of him. They snatch Dani from Max and try to kill her in front of him too. And, in a *meta* moment, they even come between Penny Marshall and her real-life brother, Garry Marshall. (The movie's theme of siblings vs. siblings might be the only plausible rationale for the otherwise befuddling choice to cast real-deal siblings as bickering husband and wife.)

The Dennison and Binx siblings' stories parallel one another. In the end, Thackery's dead body falls on top of Emily's tombstone. As he is spiritually reunited with his sister, Max is reunited — emotionally — with his. The Binxes, Sandersons, and Dennisons all go where they belong: Heaven, Hell, and home, respectively.

> **Dani:** Come on, Binx, let's go home.
> **Binx:** Home!
> **Max:** Home.

As timpani rumble and the primary storyline comes to a close, Ortega frames our siblings in a warm and joyous embrace, anchoring the story in Dani and Max.

This idea of home emerges as a major theme in the screenplay, arising at least as often as virginity. Upon their return to Salem, the Sandersons fling the front door open with an exuberant "we're home!" While trick-or-treating, Max and Dani argue over who wants to go home more (and over which place "home" means). Later, Dani excitedly tells Thackery she and her descendants are his new household. Winifred leans out her window and cries desperately for her book to "come home, or make thyself known." And on multiple occasions, the Dennisons and Sandersons break into each other's houses.

It is through defeating the witches that Max finally finds himself at home in Massachusetts, his family restored at last — and only after they die can his parents return to their house from Town Hall. Like the Wicked Witch of the West and so many of her progeny, these are witches who stand in the way of home. Incidentally, the three good fairies of *Sleeping Beauty* keep Aurora from her true home too.

There might be something to this idea, then, that independent or unmarried women in fantasy — the so-called spinsters — are presented as a threat to "home life" and the nuclear family. For that matter, the Salem

Witch Trials directly targeted real-life spinsters for the same reason.

For most of Aurora's life, Flora, Fauna, and Merryweather disguise themselves as spinsters. Likewise, when the villagers of 1693 come in search of the Binxes, the Sandersons claim to be "just three kindly old spinster ladies." And there is at least one other witchy spinster of note in the Disney canon: Eglantine Price.

The heroine of 1971's *Bedknobs and Broomsticks*, Eglantine Price (Angela Lansbury) is a prim, drably dressed, no-nonsense spinster. She doesn't have children and doesn't want any, but she's forced to care for them by government decree during World War II. Her animosity toward tykes is due in part to her personality, but it's also because she doesn't want them sniffing out her hidden hobby of apprentice witchcraft.[4]

Eglantine has a secret (she's a witch, but a good one). Flora, Fauna, and Merryweather have a secret (they're fairies, and their peasant daughter is the cursed princess). The Sandersons have a secret (they're sucking the lives out of the children of Salem). And they all live on the outskirts of town. Because, in an unenlightened world — and maybe even in an enlightened one — being different from other women means they need to hide.[5]

But when the Sandersons come back in 1993, they aren't especially careful about blending in. They're loud and proud. And when the bus driver asks them what they're after, they make no bones about it: "We desire children." These aren't mothers in the making, though. They're spinsters, unashamed.

Chapter Eleven

Run Amok (Amok, Amok) in the Magic Kingdom:
Walt Disney World's Villain Spelltacular

Halloween at Walt Disney World never felt quite right without *Hocus Pocus*. Sure, those who looked hard enough could find it: props in Planet Hollywood at the old Downtown Disney[1], a vaguely reminiscent skeleton band in the Boo-to-You Parade, and a generically soulful cover of Winifred's "I Put a Spell on You" in the background music at Mickey's Not-So-Scary Halloween Party.[2] But an annual Halloween shindig in Disney's most popular theme park without Disney's most popular Halloween movie on proud display seemed one Santa short of a Macy's parade.

Lo and behold, in 2015, Magic Kingdom made up for lost time in a big way, announcing a new main event for Mickey's Not-So-Scary Halloween Party: the Hocus Pocus Villain Spelltacular. Yes, Virginia, there is a benevolent executive within Disney Parks & Resorts.

The Spelltacular is a nighttime stage show performed in front of

Cinderella Castle, tricked (and treated) out with festive flare. The turrets glow green, purple, and orange, with spider webs, thorny hedges, and floating candelabras projected against the castle walls to spectral effect. On either end of the stage sits a glowing jack-o'-lantern, one a little silly and the other just as spooky. And in the center: a giant, steaming cauldron next to a rusted set of cemetery gates.[3] With an unmistakable cackle, Bette Midler emerges from behind them, Sarah Jessica Parker to her left and Kathy Najimy to her right.

No, wait, it isn't them, but I could have sworn... The actresses cast in these roles are uncanny twins of the film's three stars. They look like them, sound like them, sing like them, and even shuffle with their same cadence as the three huddle up and "run amok" to the front of the stage, a thrilling grand entrance that has the eager crowd going wild every time.[4]

Winifred: The Sanderson sisters are back!
Mary: We're back! Back... back where, Winnie?
Winifred: Isn't it obvious?
Mary: No.
Winfred: We're back in the living world.
Mary: The living world!
Winifred: Yes! Don't you understand? We've harnessed the magic found within this kingdom to return but for one night!
Sarah: One night's all I need!
Winifred: And we shall make it a grand night, filled with spell-binding tricks and treats... a night that will be long remembered!

I love this notion that not only is the Magic Kingdom a place where Disney characters "go to live" when their stories end, and not only are magical characters inhabitants in it, but there is apparently some sort of magic energy in the place that can bring villains back from the dead. For theme park buffs, this extends a narrative perpetuated by attractions like Dream Along with Mickey and Sorcerers of the Magic Kingdom.[5] If part of the park's thematic identity is that it is "where the magic lives," Villain Spelltacular subtly reinforces the mythos and suggests new possibilities for the ways in which various intellectual properties might intersect in the park.

But it isn't just the park the show shines a light on. Spelltacular demonstrates a deep and impressive understanding of *Hocus Pocus* — its story, its characters, and its charm. For that matter, it seems to come to many of the same inferences we've considered in this book. Let's start with the witches' motives in the Magic Kingdom.

> **Winifred**: Tell me, what year is it? ...Sisters! It's been *22* years since we last returned! ...And it's All Hallows' Eve! Our favorite time of year!
> **Mary**: Winnie, remember what happened on our last Halloween?
> **Sarah**: We turned to dust! Dust, dust, dust, dust, dust, dust, du-
> **Winifred**: Ooh! Don't remind me! ...That is why we have returned: to celebrate Halloween and throw the most villainous Halloween party this kingdom has ever seen!

So there is no chance for the Sandersons to recapture their youth this time. They seem to know the magic that's brought them back is absolutely capped at one night, with no "suck the lives out of children" clause in their contract. This time, they've returned with just one goal: "Make Halloween Great Again."

They're here to avenge All Hallows' Eve and "purify" it with villainy. How fitting that, in Winifred's mind, the best way to do that is to put on a show: the best party this side of Salem. She came back from the dead to do this. Remember her allusion to *Gypsy*'s Rose in the film. She just *has* to get this out of her.

In her Rose-ness, Winifred is a fully three-dimensional character — desperate, in a sense, and empathetic, but not because of her gender. Her motivation is even more progressive here than in the film. There isn't the slightest hint of jealousy, vanity, "cat fighting," or youth. Clearly, she has returned for something more.

The sisters' reference to their previous resurrection and death in 1993 makes this the rare Disney attraction to explicitly reference an intellectual property's year of release. Uncommon, too, is a Disney theme park acknowledging its characters' final moments in their respective films. (Beast is still a beast in Magic Kingdom, Ariel is usually still a mermaid,

Rapunzel still has long blonde hair, Darth Vader is alive and wearing his mask, etc.) By referencing the precise number of years that have passed since the film's release, Spelltacular gives its audience a nod, as if to say, "you're all twenty-some years older than when this movie came out, and *we remember you*." It is validation of the nostalgia we collectively feel for these characters, their world, and all the memories we've built while watching them over the years.

To throw their party, the sisters tells us, they'll need some help. They want to cast a spell on the kingdom, but they're missing three ingredients (a nice salute to the potion brewing in the movie *and* an effective framing device for incorporating other Disney characters). The first ingredient is "sinister shadows," and right on cue, Dr. Facilier from *The Princess and the Frog* shows up with what they need. There's real chemistry between them. Remember: Dr. Facilier was inspired, in part, by the real-life recording artist responsible for the original "I Put a Spell on You." And each of the four villains we now have on stage are well acquainted with Hell. The show makes direct reference to that idea:

> **Winifred, Mary, and Sarah** (excitedly): He's got friends on the other side!
> **Winifred**: Perhaps he knows Mother!...
> **Dr. Facilier**: Won't you shake a poor sinner's hand?
> **Winifred**: We'd *love* to.

This is some of the edgiest stuff I've seen in Magic Kingdom, and unsurprisingly, it comes by way of *Hocus Pocus*. Mickey's Not-So-Scary Halloween Party was born in response to Universal Orlando's Halloween Horror Nights, a truly terrifying and occasionally vulgar event that proves too intense even for many adults. By contrast, Mickey's shindig was always tonally whimsical. But now, with *Hocus Pocus*'s horror tinge in tow, Villain Spelltacular takes a small step toward "the other side."[6]

Helping them go there is their next guest, Oogie Boogie from *The Nightmare Before Christmas*.[7] He's a significant draw in and of himself. *Nightmare* has an enormous cult following, and its characters' rare appearances in Walt Disney World reliably command huge crowds. A few years earlier, Oogie Boogie headlined his own one-night-only show at Disney's Hollywood Studios. It says something about *Hocus Pocus*'s appeal that he is now but a supporting character in the Sanderson show. And remember: *Nightmare* is the movie Disney deemed too dark for its brand in 1993. Here again, Spelltacular's writers are demonstrating a real awareness of *Hocus Pocus*'s context and legacy, given that the movies share fundamental qualities of horror and are often discussed in tandem with one another. Incredibly, the dialogue in this scene is an argument between Oogie Boogie and the Sandersons about which of them is the scarier and more nightmare inducing — fitting discourse, indeed.[8] And in true Oogie Boogie fashion, he knows how to hit right at the soul of who they are; *he* threatens to cook and eat *them*.

Guest number three is (who else?) Maleficent, and unlike Dr. Facilier and Oogie Boogie, her reputation proceeds her.

Winifred: Oh, Maleficent! Oh great one! If we had known you would come, we would have invited you for sure!
Sarah: We are not worthy!
Mary: Oh, Maleficent! She… she is greater than I thought…

I can only assume the Sandersons learned about Maleficent while in the underworld (she does summon "all the powers of Hell" in *Sleeping Beauty*) or perhaps while frolicking in Salem back in '93. Either way, the reverence they show her here underscores Maleficent's stature as Disney's greatest villain. Perhaps Winifred is tacitly conceding that, of *all* the witches working, she isn't *quite* the worst.[9]

The ghost of Thackery Binx narrates the show, but neither Max nor Dani are anywhere to be found. That doesn't mean the show is virgin-less, though. The sisters' final ingredient is "the hair of an innocent," and they pluck it from one of the show's backup dancers. It's a very subtle exchange and almost certainly goes unnoticed by the majority of the audience, but the subtext is significant.

At the very beginning of the show, several dancers enter the stage to a slinking rendition of "Season of the Witch."[10] During that sequence, one of the dancers climbs a stage-left platform and lights successive sets of candles. Later, Sarah sings "Come, Little Children," and it puts the small squadron of backup singers — none of them children — under her spell. Mary smells the dancers as "children" too, even though they neither dress nor act like kids. Toward the end of the show, when the Sandersons can't find the hair of an innocent, she specifically turns to one of the dancers, points, and sings her song again. The dancer is entranced, walks toward Sarah, and Winifred plucks the hair from her head. It is the same dancer who lit the candle.[11]

What kind of "innocent" is this show referring to if not the same kind of "innocent" made so focal in the film? Moreover, if that's not the intention, why add this ingredient to the show at all? And why pluck that hair from the same character who's lighting all the candles?

I see you, show writers. Well done.

With the potion complete, the sisters have amassed a "glittering assemblage" of villainy on the stage. But Sarah looks at the audience and asks, "Oh, Winnie… what about *them*?"

"Leave our 'Not-So-Scary' friends to me," Winifred replies, launching into "I Put a Spell on You" at last. She's dropping a whammy on her unsuspecting audience all over again, and this time there's no graveyard battle to break it. The show ends with us "cursed" to party the rest of the night away.[12] No longer Mickey's Not-So-Scary, this is the *Hocus Pocus* Party, and that's just what we want it to be. One of Disney's best movies begets one of the parks' best shows, and all its themes come full circle with it.

Note: *Hocus Pocus Villain Spelltacular is exclusive to Mickey's Not-So-Scary Halloween Party, a hard-ticketed event not included in regular theme park admission. Tickets can be purchased at Walt Disney World Guest Relations windows and ticket booths or through the resort's website or telephone service.*

The event is available on select nights in September, October, and sometimes early November. Tickets typically become available in the spring and frequently sell out in advance.

The Spelltacular runs approximately 22 minutes. As of this printing, neither Walt Disney World FastPass+ nor Advance Dining Reservation packages are available. The show may frighten very young guests (Fear Factor: 2 out of 5).

The information in this chapter is premised on the 2015 event and stage show, as this book went to press prior to the 2016 debut of Mickey's Not-So-Scary Halloween Party.

Chapter Twelve

But Who Lit the Pop-Culture Candle?

*H*ocus Pocus knows its way around an insult. Winifred calls Billy a "maggoty-mouth peasant," and he calls her a "bucktoothed, mop-riding firefly from Hell." Those are some sick burns. Rosie O'Donnell and Donald Trump were gentler. Don Rickles was kinder at the Friars Club.

But the movie knows what it's like to be on the receiving end too. It's been made fun of more than Max at a swingers' party, with reviews ranging from "garbage" (*Vox*) and "disposable" (FilmCritic.com) to "an unholy mess" (*The New York Times*).[1] *The Baltimore Sun* said if Shakespeare had reviewed it, he'd have written, "Double, double, toil and trouble, movie stink and critic bubble / 'Hocus Pocus' has no focus / has no rhyme, has no reason / and is… out of season."[2] In the words of SNL's Jebidiah Atkinson, "*Next!*"

Well, it's like they say: if you can't take the heat, get out of the torture chamber.

Of all the names hurled *Hocus Pocus*'s way, none are as common as "cult classic," which I'll grant you isn't exactly slander. But what do we really mean by that, and is it fair to call *Hocus Pocus* one?

We sometimes use "cult classic" to describe a movie that wasn't popular at first but found an audience later. Some people simply use it as a euphemism for "weird." But at its literal core, the "cult" in "cult classic" is a reference to religious cults. In other words, audiences latch onto these movies with fanaticism resembling religious zeal, and I guess you might think of that as either an insult or a badge of honor.[3] Either way, the term tells us as much about the audience as it does the movie itself.

Some cult classics are offbeat and initially obscure. *Rocky Horror Picture Show* is the quintessential "midnight movie."[4] These are films defined by subversive social taboos, almost exclusively reserved for late-night screenings in small movie houses, where audiences engage in ritualistic customs such as throwing rice and toilet paper in the air. If that's how people watch *Hocus Pocus* in your town, I'd like to visit sometime. But for most of America, it seems safe to say *Hocus Pocus* isn't quite that kind of cult classic.[5]

Others are incredibly popular in the mainstream. *The Wizard of Oz*, *Singin' in the Rain*, *All About Eve*, and *Casablanca* are generally considered cult classics. While they are widely appreciated and enjoyed, they endure in large part because a passionate subset of their audience identifies with them *intensely*, holding them above reproach, with an almost mythical regard for the impact these movies had on their lives.

With any kind of cult film, the relationship between movie and audience really boils down to the idea that the movie is doing something different. Even if cult features adhere to conventional Hollywood narrative patterns (as in *Casablanca* and *Oz)*, on some level, they still cross a boundary — the boundaries of good taste, perhaps, or of social norms. *Casablanca* thrives on convenient plot points and unnaturally suave dialogue.[6] The lavish *Wizard of Oz* defies any notion of restraint in fantasy or aesthetic. And yet both pack an emotional wallop as they speak to fundamental themes about sacrifice, love, family, belonging, and home. They stir something within their audiences in spite of, and even because of, their disregard for boundaries.

We tend to discover cult movies as "accidental tourists."[7] Whenever we stumble upon them, we imagine we've found something rare, and we see in them a specialness others do not (or we at least *suspect* others don't — either because most of the people we know aren't very familiar with the movie or because it has been rejected by critics or at the box office).

Indeed, I've made that very kind of argument more than once in this book: *Hocus Pocus* is a special and meaningful movie, even though the critics of 1993 didn't see it. So it's probably fair to say that I am, in some sense, a *Hocus Pocus* cultist — and maybe you are too.

Unquestionably, the movie breaks rules. In disrupting social norms, it makes a direct connection with some of its largest audiences. It is perhaps no surprise that a movie primarily featuring female characters has been popular with women, or that a movie steeped in camp and starring a gay icon in Bette Midler has been popular among LGBT viewers.[8] But like *The Wizard of Oz*, I think, *Hocus Pocus* breaks rules in a way that speaks to a broader, universal audience at the same time. While children's literature has historically delved deeper into darkness than the public gives it credit for, *Hocus Pocus* manages to push that envelope, making sex, death, and the devil prominent plot points.[9]

These things surprise us, and so the movie has our attention, and then it makes an emotional connection.[10] In other words, the movie bonds with us. And so a cult is born. The cult is small at first, but as new "accidental tourists" discover it during some September or October and lose their *Hocus Pocus* virginity at long last, they unwittingly join.

As good cultists, we defend our movie. We find it very easy to excuse and even celebrate its shortcomings. *Casablanca* cultists relish in its over-the-top dialogue. (I'm one of them.) *Rocky Horror* lovers live for its weirdness. *Hocus Pocus* fans think "I Put a Spell on You" is the highlight of the movie, and we don't mind at all when straight-outta-1693 Winifred somehow knows what a driver's permit is.[11] We find it quite lovely.

But I take issue with the notion sometimes promulgated by film scholars that our affection for cult texts is "beyond all reason."[12] After all, if it is a fundamental tenet of film criticism that audiences respond to movies for a reason, it makes little sense to then say audiences *intensely* respond to cult movies for *no* reason. On the contrary, the reasons must be there, and perhaps even more acutely so, though they may be more deep-seated and bound up in subtext, thus harder to pin down.

I hope this book has helped to bring one of our contemporary cult classics, *Hocus Pocus*, into some sense of focus — perhaps for the first time. But in conceding that our love for the movie is cultish, it's worth pointing out that a movie can be a cult classic and an unmitigated classic at the same time. *Casablanca* and *The Wizard of Oz* are cases in point.

Hocus Pocus is already the former and may be on its way to becoming the latter. It's a pop-culture phenomenon, a forgotten film come back from the dead. As fans, we lit the pop-culture candle ourselves, and this time, the Sanderson sisters are sticking around for *plenty* of Halloweens to come.

Epilogue

The Case for a Sequel

In July 2012, Moviehole.net reported Walt Disney Pictures was actively developing a sequel to *Hocus Pocus* entitled *Hocus Pocus 2: Rise of the Elder-witch*.[1] The story spread like wildfire. *Huffington Post* amusingly quipped that the subtitle "instantly brought to mind spectacular visions of Betty White joining the cast as Bette Midler's slightly older sister." But Disney told *HuffPo* there was no merit to it.[2]

Then, two years later in April 2014, *The Tracking Board* reported Tina Fey and her production company, Little Stranger, were helming a *Hocus Pocus 2* for Disney, with Fey writing and maybe even starring alongside Melissa McCarthy.[3] Once again, seemingly credible news of a *Hocus Pocus* sequel rocked the 'net with Richter Scale intensity. (My own reaction on Twitter at the time went something like, "JESUS TAKE THE WHEEL.")

But the next day, Deadline.com cited an anonymous-but-reliable source claiming that while Disney was in talks with Fey for a new witch comedy, it wouldn't have anything to do with *Hocus Pocus*.[4] Confusion continued, though, when IMDb added a listing for *Hocus Pocus 2: Rise of the Elderwitch*, setting hopes high again.

The *next* year, in August 2015, a popular Facebook page by the name of *Tough Cookie Parenting* shared a fairly convincing poster for the sequel.[5] The image racked up hundreds of thousands of Facebook shares in mere hours and was, once again, covered by nearly every major entertainment news outlet.

It was around that time Bette Midler got involved, taking to Reddit and letting her fans know she and her co-stars welcomed a *Hocus Pocus* sequel with open arms. Not long after, in interviews and on her Twitter page, the star began actively encouraging fans to contact Disney in support of the sequel.

"Inundate the Disney company," Midler said, "because I have canvassed the girls and they are willing to do it, but we have no say in it, so if you want a *Hocus Pocus 2*, ask the Walt Disney Company… SISTAHS!"[6]

Every time she mentioned it, a new wave of articles would sweep the web. She and Najimy stoked the fire on Twitter too. "What's that you say?" Bette cracked, "*Fast and the Furious* has six sequels and *Hocus Pocus* has zero?"[7]

But finally, in the fall of 2015, Midler returned to her fans with bad news during a live online Q&A: "After all these years and all the fan demand, I do believe I can stand and firmly say an unequivocal no."[8] The same month, Kirschner confirmed Disney had passed on his pitch for a theatrical sequel a few years earlier, though he floated the possibility that Disney Channel might still pick it up as a TV movie.[9] A few days later, Sarah Jessica Parker seemed to put a big kibosh on the whole thing, telling *Vulture* talk of a sequel wasn't based in reality.[10]

Still, the speculation didn't end, ultimately inspiring Snopes.com to launch a webpage on the matter.[11] Their rumor verdict: false.

It looked like all hope was lost. But then Tina Fey popped up with a meager ray of hope. When a journalist at the Tribeca Film Festival asked about her involvement in a potential *Hocus Pocus* remake or sequel, Fey remained tightlipped, saying only this: "There is a script in development; it is not so much a remake."[12]

Not so much? Tina Fey, you tease.

Had *Hocus Pocus* been as popular in 1993 as it is today, we probably would have had a sequel by 1994. Look no further than Disney's *Sister Act*, a mammoth success in 1992 followed by 1993's fast-tracked *Back in the Habit*. (Najimy filmed *Hocus Pocus* in between the two *Sister Acts*, promoting the former while still shooting the latter.)

And the movie *might* have been that successful in 1993 had Disney not chosen an incredibly odd window for its release. While picking premiere dates is always a complex challenge for studios, it doesn't take an MBA to figure out Halloween movies won't fare as well in the summer as in the fall. Nevertheless, *Hocus Pocus* went to theaters in the middle of July, in a busy season and on the same day as *Free Willy*.[13] It's like they made the movie's tombstone alongside its press kit.

In fairness, it was a hectic year on Disney's calendar. Even without a major animated feature, 1993 welcomed several dozen new movies across the studio's various live-action divisions.[14] And there was precedent for warm-weather witchery: *The Witches of Eastwick*, while not a Halloween story, had been fairly successful in mid-June 1987. But more than anything, the studio likely wanted to keep October open for *The Nightmare Before Christmas*. So things didn't work out for *Hocus Pocus* right away.

Would we have wanted them to? Winifred's spell book opening its eye at the end credits is a sequel tease on the order of Marvel, but do we *really* want one?[15] While *Sister Act 2* has an almost cult following all its own, the general consensus is it falls short of the original. The same goes for the overwhelming majority of sequels. *Hocus Pocus*'s story is self-contained and satisfactorily resolved. Could a follow-up possibly recapture "the magic" or add something new? *Especially* a quarter-century later? Maybe passing on the project is Disney's way of saying "thou wouldst hate us in the morning." Perhaps we wouldst.

Two things justify a sequel's existence: an audience that wants to spend more time in its universe and a story that makes that time worthwhile. The first of those factors clearly weighs in *Hocus Pocus 2*'s favor. But what about the latter?

Undoubtedly, there are questions left unanswered. What was the Sandersons' deal in the 1690s? How did they become witches? What happened to their mother? What was their plan after they acquired youthful immortality? What did Thackery do during these intervening 300 years? What becomes of Jay and Ice? How much sentience and power does the spell book really have? Did the black-flame candle completely melt? What happened to the three little girls who stole the flying brooms? Does Max ever take Dani trick-or-treating as a tights-wearing Peter Pan? Are the Sandersons really gone for good?

I'd like answers to those questions. So would millions of others, I gather. A *Hocus Pocus* sequel would seem to be a surefire, mid-sized hit — not a colossal blockbuster, but with the right budget in place, a moneymaker. Once upon a time, Disney had an interest in those kinds of returns. But in the Iger era, the studio's focus is almost exclusively on larger, franchise-oriented tentpoles, and that's the biggest obstacle. Still, if *Into the Woods* can get a green light, maybe a new Sanderson romp can too.[16]

It needn't be a sequel in the conventional sense (though *E! News* sketched a plot for one, with Winifred's spell book stored away in grown-up Max and Allison's attic, waiting for their mischievous kids to find it).[17] A remake is always a possibility, maybe as a full-fledged musical. For their part, *Playbill* drew up elaborate plans for a Broadway adaptation.[18]

A prequel seems promising too. There's a lot of backstory to fill in, and nearly a quarter-century later, Midler, Parker, and Najimy could still play the pre-Binx Sandersons of 1693.[19]

Of course, these days, Hollywood is all aflutter with the "legacyquel," a very specific kind of sequel in which aging stars reprise beloved roles to simultaneously remake and advance their stories (*TRON: Legacy, Star Wars: The Force Awakens*, etc.), often passing the baton to a younger generation at the end. I think a different kind of "legacyquel" might be the best bet for *Hocus Pocus*, though — one we haven't seen a whole lot of in Hollywood.

Sleepless in Seattle hit theaters exactly three weeks prior to *Hocus Pocus*, and the two competed against each other at the box office. Marc Shaiman worked on both films, and had Rosie O'Donnell taken the role of Mary Sanderson, she would have been up against herself at the box office that year. *Sleepless*'s most important connection isn't to a 1993 movie, though, but a 1957 one: *An Affair to Remember*. After watching the old black-and-white classic, Annie (Meg Ryan) feels inspired to write a love letter to Sam (Tom Hanks), and rom-com shenanigans ensue. In this way, the events of *Sleepless in Seattle* are driven almost entirely by *An Affair to Remember*. It's not so much a sequel or a remake, but it absolutely seizes *An Affair*'s legacy and runs with it. The events of the '93 movie transpire because the '57 movie exists within its characters' world.

We see something similar in *Rumor Has It* (2005, featuring yet another score by Marc Shaiman).[20] Sarah (Jennifer Aniston) discovers that her grandmother (Shirley MacLaine) might have been the inspiration for Mrs. Robinson in *The Graduate* (both the 1963 novella and the 1967 film). Though entirely fictional, the story uses *The Graduate* as a springboard for an original comedy, one very much wrapped up in the culture's aware-ness and love of a classic. *Jersey Girl* (2004) has a similar relationship with Stephen Sondheim's *Sweeney Todd*.

Those are all romantic comedies, and *Hocus Pocus* isn't one, but the con-cept might have some utility here nevertheless. Whatever the approach, the project's success would ultimately hinge on its script. We can only hope some crackerjack screenwriter has a lightning bolt of an idea. Maybe that screenwriter is Tina Fey: brilliant, '90s-inclined, and clearly inter-ested in putting women in strong leading roles.

Whether prequel, midquel, sequel, remake, or "loosely inspired by," there is unquestionably a wick here waiting for the right flame. The Sand-ersons stood by for 300 years, counting on a full-mooned Halloween night with an audacious virgin. By those standards, our vigil for a new movie is young, and there's still plenty of wax left in this pop-culture candle. The fans may resurrect the Sandersons yet. And when they do, the perfect tagline awaits them: "The witch is back, and there's hell to pay."

Afterword

By Mick Garris

Back in 1986, when I first met with David Kirschner to discuss his idea for a playfully frightening movie called *Halloween House*, nobody imagined that it would become a perennial media icon, that Halloweens all across the country would be rife with girls in Sanderson sisters costumes and boys shambling about as Bad Billy Butcherson. David had originally made his mark by creating a cartoon series called "Strawberry Shortcake" before creating and producing the wonderful animated feature, *An American Tale*, with Steven Spielberg. At the time, I too was working with Spielberg, on the first job in a brand-new screenwriting career: Story Editor on Steven's series, "Amazing Stories."

David spins a wonderful tale, and his pitch to me was filled with enthusiasm and magic and awe, glimmering with memories of youth and fear and witches and bags of candy. I was immediately captivated by it and came on board at once.

We actually proposed the film to Steven himself; I remember how David had dressed the conference room before the meeting with all the accouterments of Halloween and autumn, covering the meeting table with a cornucopia of seasonal goods, setting the lighting in its moodiest mode, and actually creating the setting of storytelling as the sun goes down on All Hallows' Eve.

As is reported in this very book you hold in your hands, Steven chose not to be a part of what was to become *Hocus Pocus*, as his company was getting its own slate in place, and, honestly, I don't think that he wanted to be in the Disney business at that time.

But what an adventure it became!

Once I signed on, the studio arranged a research trip to Salem, Massachusetts, to this day the home of more self-proclaimed witches than anywhere else in the world. I was delighted to find that Salem is a place that revels in its past and in fact celebrates every year with a ten-day festival of sorcery and the macabre, climaxing on Halloween night with a candlelight vigil to Gallows Hill, where the "witches" of the Salem Witch Trials were executed in 1692. Oddly festive for such a melancholy event, it's a really remarkable, unique experience. I was so excited by it that I returned another half dozen Halloweens, just for the fun of it.

Once I'd experienced modern Salem, and sparked by Kirschner's ideas, the script practically wrote itself. We thought we were off to the races... and production would be imminent.

Oh, how wrong we were.

It would be eight years between the time I turned in my script and the day it began production. Eight years... and another bunch of writers whose hands the screenplay ran through before it was made. It's not uncommon for multiple writers to become involved in a studio project, and Disney was famous for being a leader in the multiply employed, but this was a big number even for the House of the Mouse. A total of a dozen writers worked on *Hocus Pocus*, for who-knows-what reasons. So when, eight years after I had turned in my final draft, I got word that the studio had gotten Bette Midler (then at the height of her career) to star in the film, and that they were ready to start shooting, I was shocked and delighted — especially when I learned that so much of what I had done in the months I worked on it was maintained in the shooting script.

And they were off and running!

There were changes from what I had originally written (with another

11 writers' contributions, how could there not be?). My original draft, and the approach David and I had started with, was about twelve-year-olds rather than the high schoolers the film ended up being about. For me, Halloween is its most potent at that age, that awkward step between childhood and maturity, when that dark holiday is truly a turning point in the process of growing up. Like *Stand by Me*, it felt more deeply rooted in life at that age. But the studio apparently felt differently, and the characters aged overnight (well, over the course of the next eight years, anyway). And although we had always intended to make it playfully creepy, what I had originally written was a few degrees darker and a little less slapstick.

But guess what? It ended up the studio, commercially at least, was right! Although the film was only a modest success at the time of its release, over the last couple of decades, it seems to have become a seminal film for a vast audience.

I can only guess why it seems to have struck such a strong chord, particularly in female audiences. The Sanderson sisters were brought vividly to life by an amazing assortment of actresses who brought so much humor and personality to the film: Bette Midler still claims to this day that it was her favorite role ever. Sarah Jessica Parker and Kathy Najimy are at the height of their considerable comedic powers. It's about a turning point, a growing-up process that almost all of us can identify with, and it strikes an emotional place in the heart when we experience loss.

Many of Disney's most classic films were pretty bold in the darkness of their visions. How many children were traumatized by the loss of Bambi's mother in the fire? And the death of Old Yeller? I know I was.

But it's also a story of magic, vividly and colorfully brought to life by director Kenny Ortega, who, before *Hocus Pocus*, was known mainly as a choreographer. It plays with our precepts of love and fear, of life and loss, but frames it in a joyous, comic celebration of my favorite holiday. It offers the opportunity to play tag with our fears... but from a safe distance.

Halloween has become much more important to American culture in the decades since *Hocus Pocus* came out, which, other than its commercial exploitation, is a good thing. How wonderful to don a costume, to reimagine ourselves as colorful characters, wearing the masks of our choice. To be whoever we want to be. And, at least for that one night of the year, to run amok, amok, amok...

About Mick Garris

Mick Garris's big break came when Steven Spielberg hired him as writer and story editor for "Amazing Stories," an anthology series that brought Spielberg's signature blend of fantasy, science fiction, and horror to NBC airwaves weekly from 1985 to 1987.

Impressed with his work, Spielberg tapped Garris to direct an episode of "Stories," and he has been writing, producing, and editing ever since. His efforts on that show even won him an Edgar Award, reserved for outstanding works of mystery created in the tradition of Edgar Allen Poe.

Garris's work also includes *batteries not included* (1987), "Freddy's Nightmares" (1988), *Critters 2* (1988), "Tales from the Crypt" (1989), *The Fly II* (1989), *Psycho IV: The Beginning* (1990), *Hocus Pocus* (1993), *Virtual Obsession* (1998), *The Judge* (2001), and *Lost in Oz* (2002).

Stephen King opened the next chapter in Garris's career when he hired him to direct the renowned author's original screenplay, *Sleepwalkers*, in 1992. In the years since, King has called on Garris again and again to adapt and/or direct his work for screens big and small. He helmed 1994's "The Stand," which became one of the most watched programs in television history, and a three-part, mini-series adaptation of King's *The Shining* in 1997. Their other projects together include *Quicksilver Highway* (1997), *Riding the Bullet* (2004), *Desperation* (2006), and *Bag of Bones* (2011).

A master of horror himself, Garris created the acclaimed Showtime series, "Masters of Horror," in 2005, followed by the spin-off anthology series, "Fear Itself." Those shows, in turn, paved the way for "Post Mortem," a horror genre-themed talk show on FearNetHD, with Garris as host and creator. Garris offers many of these and his other interviews with horror legends for public access at MickGarrisInterviews.com.

He has directed episodes for a number of popular television series, including "Pretty Little Liars," "Ravenswood," and "Witches of East End." He also executive produced *Unbroken* (2014), directed by Angelina Jolie.

Garris's novels include *Development Hell, Snow Shadows, Tyler's Third Act, Salome,* and *Ugly*. He is also the author of *A Life in Cinema*, a short story collection. Additionally, Garris sits on the board of advisors at the Hollywood Horror Museum. In 2006, the New York Horror Film Festival honored him with its Lifetime Achievement Award. Several new Mick Garris series and features are in development as this book goes to press.

Bonus Material

Fun Facts
and Additional Observations:

Everything You Never Knew About *Hocus Pocus*

The Story

The idea for *Hocus Pocus* came to creator David Kirschner while sitting outside with his daughter at night. A neighbor's cat crawled by, and he began to weave a story about a young boy who, 300 years ago, was trying to save his sister from three witches when they turned him into a cat for eternity. His daughter was enthralled.[1]

Recognizing the potential in his off-the-cuff bedtime tale, Kirschner penned a short story and published it in *Muppet Magazine*. The strong response told him there was something to the idea, and so he decided to develop a feature film treatment.

Mick Garris came aboard to expand the story with feature-length scope. Among other things, he fleshed out the characters, gave them names, and developed the story of Billy Butcherson.

To get Disney on board, Kirschner decorated a conference room with the sights and sounds of Halloween. He poured 15 pounds of candy corn around a cauldron filled with dry ice and put children's sketches of black cats on the walls. He fixed two brooms and an Electrolux vacuum cleaner to the ceiling. "My purpose was for them to smell Halloween," he said, "to smell their childhood."[2]

The film's financial prospects had Disney's attention. Kirschner explained that, by the mid-80s, Halloween had grown into a nearly $3 billion industry, and yet there were relatively few Halloween movies for families. The time was ripe for one, he argued. They agreed.[3]

Kirschner left the meeting but hadn't even reached his car in the parking lot when one of the Disney suits came running after him. "Don't take it anywhere else," he said. "We want to do it."[4]

Originally entitled *Halloween House*, the movie was intended as a Disney Channel Premiere Film (what we would now call a Disney Channel Original Movie). But Disney Studios Chairman Jeffrey Katzenberg held the project close to his heart. As big names continued to attach, it became clear this movie was destined for the big screen.

In Garris and Kirschner's hands, the story was fairly dark. Katzenberg needed other writers to retool it before he could give it the go-ahead. Many tried, but it was playwright Neil Cuthbert who successfully enhanced the script's comedic tone and added just a dash of outrageousness, getting a green light from Disney at long last.[5]

History

Halloween 1993 fell on a Sunday, so school wouldn't have been in session. I doubt anyone was even thinking about that when the movie premiered in July. But the story didn't get its entire timeline wrong: October 31 really was the first day of Daylight Saving Time in 1993.

Full-moon Halloweens are very rare. There was one in 1955 and 2001 but not in 1993. The next will be in 2020.

The Salem Witch Trials officially ended in May 1693. Word must not have reached the Sandersons' neighborhood in time for their hanging five months later. Then again, the sisters' execution wasn't so much a trial as a vigilante mob's summary judgment.

At one point, Mary Sanderson seems to say, "Scrod... you know, it's a bottom dweller. You cook it sometimes, with a little bit of bread crumbs, little bit of margarine or oil..." There is a theory among some fans that Mary is actually referencing marjoram (an herb), not margarine (which did not exist in 1693). It's a funny line, either way.

Casting

The role of Max Dennison was originally offered to Leonardo DiCaprio. He later told *Variety* Disney offered him "more money than I ever dreamed of," but he made the difficult decision to co-star with Johnny Depp in *What's Eating Gilbert Grape* (1993) instead.[6] The critically acclaimed role ultimately paved a path toward stardom for DiCaprio and earned him his first Oscar nod.

Had Dicaprio taken the part, it would have marked a reunion with Thora Birch. They appeared together in the 1990-91 TV series, "Parenthood."

Omri Katz didn't get the role at first. He was sick during his first audition, and the filmmakers turned him down. But Katz stood out, and Ortego & Co. invited him to a redo. He landed the part after all.

The role of Mary Sanderson was originally offered to Rosie O'Donnell, who reportedly turned it down because she didn't like the idea of playing a witch who kills children. She made *Another Stakeout* for Touchstone instead. Birch later co-starred with O'Donnell in *Now and Then* (1995).

Kathy Najimy, too, was concerned about the potentially anti-feminist implications of playing a witch, as well as the risk of offending actual witches. Conflicted, she sought advice from feminist icon Gloria Steinem, who persuaded Najimy that a "child-eating witch" was, in her view, empowering. The myth of witches who ate children began with spinsters who sometimes doubled as colonial healthcare providers and performed abortions. Women would enter these spinster cottages while pregnant and then exit post-pregnancy, leading townspeople to fear the spinsters were consuming babies inside. Najimy, outspokenly pro-choice, felt justified in taking the role. She also worked closely with producers and Kenny Ortega to avoid overtly pejorative stereotypes against women, including witches.[7]

In 1979, a young Sarah Jessica Parker starred in the title role of *Annie* in the Alvin Theatre (now the Neil Simon Theatre) on Broadway. At the same time, Bette Midler was headlining a Broadway show of her own, *Bette! Divine Madness* in the Majestic Theatre. Parker looked up to the brassy star down the street, and the two shared the same vocal coach at the time, despite the twenty-year age gap between them. Parker would arrive at her lessons early so she could eavesdrop on Midler's warm-up sessions and mimic the diva's regiment. Years later, she accepted the part in *Hocus Pocus* largely because it meant a chance to work with one of her idols.

Najimy was a big Midler fan too — so much so she describes herself as a "crazy sycophant." She once jumped backstage at the Hollywood Bowl and dashed to Midler's dressing room, all in the hopes of meeting her. On another occasion, she broke into a gate at Midler's apartment and left the star a note of admiration. Later, she dressed as a bunny and delivered a singing telegram to Bette backstage at The Greek Theatre in Los Angeles (a nod to one of Midler's famous scenes in 1988's *Beaches*). She collected every album, decorated her walls with magazine clippings, and even made Bette the star on her Christmas tree. Needless to say, she took the chance to play Midler's sister in a movie without a moment's hesitation.[8]

Hocus Pocus marked two consecutive "Mary" roles at the Disney studio for Najimy. A year earlier, she'd found her big breakthrough in *Sister Act* (1992), delighting audiences as Sister Mary Patrick. She sang in both movies. Interestingly, the lead role of Deloris Van Cartier (then named Terri Van Cartier) had originally been offered to Midler, who turned it down, fearing that playing a nun would be too much a mismatch for her "divine" public persona. The role went to Whoopi Goldberg instead, and the script was retooled for Goldberg's particular talents. Midler, who assisted in story development in *Sister Act*'s early stages, later regretted passing on the project. But remnants of her involvement remain. Two of Midler's 1990s "Harlettes" (her real-life backup singers), Charlotte Crossley and Jenifer Lewis, starred as Goldberg's backup singers in the film. (Lewis went on to become a star in her own right, appearing in several projects with Goldberg and Midler and later providing the voice of Flo in Disney/Pixar's *Cars* and Mama Odie in *The Princess and the Frog*.)

Midler and Parker co-starred in *The First Wives Club* (1996), marking their second movie together. Dame Maggie Smith joined them, having also starred in the *Sister Act*s with Kathy Najimy earlier in the decade.

In a 2010 episode of "Who Do You Think You Are?" Sarah Jessica Parker learned her tenth great-grandmother, Esther Elwell, had been accused of witchcraft while living in Salem. Not only did she survive unharmed, it was Elwell's case that formally brought the Salem Witch Trials to an end, just five months before Sarah Sanderson was to have been hanged outside her home in *Hocus Pocus*'s Salem. Oddly, the episode made no mention of Parker's work in *Hocus Pocus*, but the coincidence is astounding.

Veteran character actress Kathleen Freeman plays Max and Allison's teacher, Mrs. Olin. Freeman is perhaps best remembered as Lina Lamont's diction coach, Phoebe Dinsmore, in *Singin' in the Rain* (1952). Freeman's co-star, Debbie Reynolds, later starred in *Halloweentown*, another Disney Halloween favorite.

Comedian Charles Rocket plays Max and Dani's dad, Dave Dennison. Rocket was well known for using an unscripted F-word during a live broadcast of "Saturday Night Live" in 1981. (He was fired from the show shortly thereafter.) When his character tells Max to watch his language in *Hocus Pocus*, it's a tongue-in-cheek nod to the scandal.

Jodie-Amy Rivera, who plays one of the three little girls who swipe the Sandersons' brooms, was an unknown child actress in 1993. Today, she's a popular YouTuber, racking up millions of views at a time on her channel, VenetianPrincess. Until 2012, her account had more YouTube subscribers than any other with a woman in the lead. (Scores of internet articles, even from reputable publications, inaccurately report VenetianPrincess played Emily Binx, causing a great deal of confusion for both actresses online.)

Though it is Sean Murray who appears on-screen as Thackery Binx, Jason Marsden provides the character's voice in both his human and feline forms. So even when Murray's mouth moves, it's Marsden's voice we hear.

Much of the shooting had wrapped by the time Ortega asked Marsden to dub Thackery. The black cat animatronics had already been animated to match Murray's voice, not Marsden's, but the filmmakers decided Thackery should have an old-world voice instead of Murray's more contemporary inflection.[9]

Marsden originally read for the role of Max.

Katz had previously worked with Marsden in "Eerie, Indiana," and the two remain close friends today. While *Hocus Pocus* was in production, Marsden was already at work on the Disney lot, filming "Boy Meets World" on a nearby soundstage. Though Katz had edged him out for the role of Max, Marsden still ventured over to the *Hocus Pocus* set to hang out with his buddy between shoots — and all of this *before* Marsden was hired for Thackery. In fact, it might have been Marsden's time on the set that helped him get that part.[10]

Today, Marsden enjoys a reputation as an actor who was in "everything millennials love."[11]

Murray made his big-screen debut three months earlier in *This Boy's Life*, starring Leonardo DiCaprio.

Marsden and Murray remain friends today too.[12]

Ortega led an exhaustive casting process to find the right Max and Allison. He likened the search for Max to the casting call in *Newsies*. "We saw over 600 boys," he said.[13]

Vinessa Shaw was relatively new to acting, but she'd earned acclaim as a young model. Ortega felt confident in her as a perfect fit for the character.

The search for Dani was much shorter. Thora Birch quickly rose to the top of the casting pool, and there was little question in the filmmakers' minds. Ortega called her one of the top five children in her age group. "She is a very dynamic little girl," he said, "and once we met her, we knew she was our Dani."[14]

Birch was no stranger to holiday movies, having already starred in *All I Want for Christmas* (1991) and the sci-fi comedy, *Purple People Eater* (1988).

The Characters

Max also happens to be Kirschner's middle name. He created the character as a more adventuresome *alter ego* for himself.

Kirschner named Binx after Inks, a black cat he had taken care of as a boy. It's not the same cat he saw with his daughter the night he developed *Hocus Pocus*, though. (That cat was named Sam.)

Neither the story treatment nor the screenplay provided much in the way of background information about the three witches. Ortega invited the stars to create the characters for themselves, informed by the dialogue.

Parker saw Sarah as the most fundamentally evil of the three. "Because she is so not bright, so not calculating... it is her innate nature to be evil," she said. "[With her] older sisters, it's a learned thing, it's like learning to like liver. They have, like, *learned* this evil, and I have just picked it up as part of my environment, and so I wanted her to be truly evil in the most uncalculating way and still somehow be seductive."[15] She drew inspiration from Shakespeare's nymphs and Vladimir Nabokov's *Lolita*, with "a bit of a half-wit thrown in."[16]

Parker worked hard on developing the right voice for Sarah. She tried several affectations on for size. First, she replicated "Saturday Night Live" star Dana Carvey's impression of singer George Michael — only she did it as a four-year-old English schoolboy. She loved it, but no one else on the set did. The next idea was to go for a Marilyn Monroe-type voice, but Parker felt it was boring, too whispery, and cliché. Finally, she landed on a voice in between — a seductive kind of stupid. She later compared the voice to a small child on helium.[17]

Najimy based her character, in part, on Eddie Haskell, the notorious suck-up in TV's "Leave it to Beaver." "She wants to be part of the power club," Najimy said, "and Winifred's got the power."[18]

Mary Sanderson's distinctive hair was Najimy's idea. During rehearsals, she spotted a pumpkin from the art department. It had an enormous stem that curled as it rose, with a twist at the top. She asked for a wig to resemble that shape, hoping her shadow would immediately suggest Halloween. As she describes it, the wig "looks like it's a branch growing out of my head with spiders and dirt."[19]

Midler conducted her own research to come up with the right look, demeanor, and sound. She sifted through countless stories, photographs, and prosthetics. Her goal was to create a distinctive "signature" witch that would stand out from any other.

Choreographer Peggy Holmes asked Midler, Parker, and Najimy to drive a car while she rode in the passenger seat. She studied the way each gripped the wheel and noticed interesting distinctions. She then worked with the actresses to develop a characteristic manner of mounting, riding, and gripping their brooms, based on the way they drive. The actresses also worked with the crew to develop unique postures and gaits.[20]

"Each actress flew in character," Holmes said. "Winifred is in charge and much more aggressive than the other two. She's always leading the way and looking for children. Sarah loves to fly. She's always lifting up with her mop and can't wait to get up in the air, whereas Mary is more cautious. Like a good driver, she signals with her hand. Mary is the safe and steady flier."

Ortega asked the three leads to conceive of themselves as an established acting trio.

The creators envisioned Billy Butcherson as a regal aristocrat in his time, "a ghoulish version of Ichabod Crane."

Billy went by several names as the story developed. Winifred uses one of the older iterations in the film. Listen closely to hear her say "Billy the Butcher" while standing outside the cemetery.

Billy's tombstone tells us he died on May 1, 1693, meaning Winifred murdered him around the same time the Salem Witch Trials came to an end (and just five months before she and her sisters killed Emily).

When Mary says, "Winifred, thou art divine," Najimy is making an in-joke, acknowledging Midler's nickname, "The Divine Miss M."

As commentator Kelvin Cedeño has noted, there is some narrative symmetry in the characters' climactic showdown. Max, who'd gone trick-or-treating as a little leaguer earlier, defends himself with a baseball bat in the graveyard. Billy, who has been misunderstood because Winifred sewed his mouth shut, now outwits her by unleashing a verbal diatribe as a means of distraction.[21]

The Crew

Among the film's several co-producers is Bonnie Bruckheimer, former wife of longtime Disney producer Jerry Bruckheimer and a partner in Midler's All Girl Productions. Bruckheimer is best known as producer for a slew of Midler projects, including *Bette Midler No Frills*, *Big Business*, *Beaches*, *Stella*, *For the Boys*, *Gypsy*, *That Old Feeling*, *Diva Las Vegas*, and TV's "Bette." As an actress, she appears alongside Midler in her "Seinfeld" episode ("The Understudy") and as herself in "We Are the World: The Story Behind the Song." She is also credited as an associate of Ms. Milder on *Jinxed*. Apart from Disney and Midler, Bruckheimer is known for producing *The Divine Secrets of the Ya-Ya Sisterhood* (2002).

Cedeño (above), along with commentator Albert Gutierrez, notes that in addition to his work on many Midler projects, Marc Shaiman also scored two major projects Midler turned down: *Misery* (1990) and *Sister Act*. Emile Ardolino, who had previously worked with Ortega in *Dirty Dancing*, directed the latter. Ardolino went on to direct Midler's *Gypsy*. It was his final project before passing away due to complications of AIDS on November 20, 1993.

Ortega had previously worked with Bette Midler on *The Rose*. It was the feature film debut for both.

Hocus Pocus is the only movie Ortega has directed but not choreographed. (He does take second billing for choreography in the film's end credits, but Holmes was the film's principal choreographer.)

Special Effects

SFX teams created more than a dozen Audio-Animatronics for feline Thackery Binx, one for each manner of motion required. His facial expressions were added later, using some of the most advanced CGI technology ever used in a film production at that time.

A special effects company called Rhythm & Hues Studios performed the primary computer animation, though the people at Pixar also played a part.

Hocus Pocus was the first feature-length project for Rhythm & Hues. Their work on Binx paved the way for their efforts in *Babe* (1995), which won the company its first Oscar. Rhythm & Hues went on to become one of the preeminent providers of animated special effects in the global film industry.

Disney deemed Rhythm & Hues's first design for Thackery's face too scary. It featured sharp fangs and a generally intense expression. The studio asked for a friendlier face with softer, shorter teeth instead.

While the movie was an early leader in implementing CGI in live-action, the majority of its special effects are practical in nature, lending a sense of classical style to the production.

Flight plays a big role in the story, and so the project was ambitious from the start. While detailed puppets were created for wide shots, most of the flying scenes feature the three principal actresses themselves. It would have been safer and easier to rely more heavily on stunt doubles and wide shots, but the illusion of flight would not have been nearly so convincing.

Midler, Parker, and Najimy spent many hours in harnesses, often having to shoot one take after another to get the rhythm of flight just right. While the actresses all seemed to have fun, they had to endure significant discomfort and pain. Midler suffered moderate back injuries and had to seek treatment from a chiropractor after shooting.

In close-up shots, like those used for Sarah's song, the actresses were able to sit in more comfortable teeter rigs instead.

The wire work used on *Hocus Pocus*'s mops, vacuums, and brooms is the same developed by Disney visual effects master Danny Lee for *Bedknobs and Broomsticks*. Lee utilized similar effects in *Mary Poppins* (1964) and *Pete's Dragon* (1977).

The harnesses were suspended from moving tracks fixed to the ceilings. The tracks were inspired by those used in Disneyland's dark rides.

When Billy opens his mouth, the moths that fly out are *real*. To nail the scene, Jones held live moths inside his mouth until it was time to release them. (A dental dam kept him from accidentally swallowing them.) Talk about dedication to your craft!

Behind the Scenes

Known for her improvisational skills, Najimy brought an atmosphere of trial and error to the set. Midler and Najimy improvised a number of their lines and tried many different readings of the script.[22]

While filming, Midler asked stagehands to pitch her lingo from dictionaries of old curse words.[23]

Sarah Sanderson's hair alternates between curly and straight without explanation, perhaps in homage to Dorothy's famously inconsistent hair length in *The Wizard of Oz* (1939).

Another reference to *Oz* turns up when Winifred says to Max, "You have no powers here!" Glinda makes a similar remark to the Wicked Witch of the West.

Many scenes were left on the cutting room floor. During her press tour, Sarah Jessica Parker said she felt surprised and even disappointed upon seeing the final cut because so much of her work had been edited out. (Though disappointed, she ultimately remained supportive of the editing process.)[24]

Kenny Ortega and costume designer Mary Vogt made a conscious decision to avoid black costumes, green faces, and typical witch apparel. They wanted their characters to look lively, colorful, and autumnal.

Sarah's wardrobe was designed to be light, fluid, and sexy. Vogt based the design on early twentieth-century dancers, including Agnes DeMille, Isadora Duncan, and Ruth St. Denis.

Vogt envisioned Mary as an herbalist who stayed home to cook up potions. The rings on her belt are there so she could hang herbs, dead rodents, and other ingredients for easy access. (Incidentally, this fact might lend some credence to the "marjoram" theory described under "History" above.)

Disney executives asked makeup artist Tony Gardner to tone down Billy's makeup, as they feared it might be too scary.

To get into character as Billy, Doug Jones had to undergo two-and-a-half hours of makeup application every day. His getup included foam latex over his entire face and neck, a full body suit to give him an exaggerated zombie body structure, long gloves with acrylic finger extensions, a ratty wig, and large shoes with fake toes protruding through them. His eye makeup was inspired by *Bambi* — innocent, expressive, and doe-eyed. The filmmakers wanted him to strike a balance between handsome and grotesque.

Jones is only in the Billy suit while his head is "on." Headless Billy is portrayed by actresss Karyn Malchus. At 5'4", she fit nicely into the suit, wearing shoe lifts to put her in just the right position.

In the original script, Billy Butcherson called Winifred "bitch" instead of "wench" and, on another occasion, referred to the sisters as "those bitches." The decision to change the line was actor Doug Jones's, not Disney's. Jones went on to script Billy's diatribe in that scene himself.

Jones has said many of the movie's followers have written to him and relayed that, as young fans, Billy Butcherson was their first crush.

Beauty and the Beast isn't the only Disney movie to inspire a Salemite costume in the film. During the Town Hall dance party, eagle-eyed viewers can spot a townsperson in a *TRON* suit (likely from the actual film wardrobe, borrowed from the Disney Archives).

Many of the other party costumes in that scene were on loan from

Columbia/TriStar's 1985 *Alice in Wonderland* miniseries. Look for the Mad Hatter (originally worn by Anthony Newley), March Hare (originally worn by Roddy McDowall), several playing cards, and the King of Hearts (originally worn by Robert Morley).

Among the trick-or-treating children, you can also find a kid dressed as *Halloween*'s Michael Myers.

"What's wonderful," Kirschner said during the production, "is that this work is bringing out the child in all of these people who, as adults, are quite brilliant. But what they're able to do now is combine these childhood memories with the imaginations that they have today."[25]

Alternate and Deleted Scenes

A preview for the VHS release offers a brief glimpse of just three deleted scenes: Winifred calling trick-or-treaters "greedy little beggars," Mary and Sarah blaming each other for pushing Winifred into the high school swimming pool, and an undoubtedly hilarious scene with the sisters shopping in a grocery store. The theatrical trailer also includes a scene in which the sisters peer into a student's locker after hours. Sadly, none of these scenes were included on the VHS or any subsequent home video release.

The scenes were likely deleted because they conformed to an earlier version of the story in which the Sandersons were evil candymakers. They lured their prey to the cottage by leaving trails of magical candy crows, which entranced children upon consumption. (Incidentally, had that version of the story survived, it might have provided an alternative explanation for the movie's strangely selective spell — only those who eat are cursed.)

Billy featured in several deleted scenes too, including an extended dance sequence during "I Put a Spell on You" and a graveyard come-on to his former lover, Sarah Sanderson.

The grocery store scene involved the witches gathering ingredients for their candies. According to an earlier version of the script, Mary was to down a bottle of witch hazel and mistake a can of Gerber for an actual canned baby.

Other alternate scenes would have included Winifred "surfing" on her broom while Beach Boys music plays (during her attempt to pull Max over while driving); Winifred exclaiming, "The witch is back" after walking out of the furnace; the good guys hiding out in a pumpkin patch; Allison's friends eating the witches' candy, and a telephone conversation in The Master's house. Several stretches of dialogue with Mr. and Mrs. Dennison (most of it generic filler) were excised as well.

When Winifred teases Max about his driver's permit, it is a callback to a deleted storyline in which Max was stressed over not having one.

An earlier version of the script suggested Allison is the descendant of good witches and may even be a witch herself. Mary was to have eaten one of Allison's ancestors.

An alternate ending would have seen Thackery return to life and go home with Dani as an ordinary housecat, followed by a "big moment" kiss between Allison and Max.

One of my favorite sequences from the supposedly deleted material includes this quip by Mary during the hanging scene, spoken to a villager while in the noose: "Did I leave the cauldron burning? Would thou mindst checking if I left the cauldron burning?"

Several fans have tracked down remnants of old scripts and unused production or publicity stills and posted them online, but how much of the material was ever filmed and/or has been preserved is unclear.[26] At any rate, the Disney Company likely has a wealth of unreleased material at its disposal.

In 2015, the "Wonderful World of Disney" presented *Mary Poppins* on ABC with special interstitials hosted by Dick Van Dyke. The legendary entertainer strolled through aisles of what purported to be a Disney Studios archives room, where movie props and unopened crates from popular movies filled massive shelves. One of those crates was clearly labeled "*Hocus Pocus.*" Fans hoped the studio was dropping a hint, but at what was never clear. (Attention, Disney: please unearth these sequences — and any of the other gems in your treasure chest — and issue a *Hocus Pocus*: Deluxe Edition Blu-ray at long last!)

The Set and Locations

Most of the scenes were shot on Stage 2 at the Disney Studios in Burbank, the company's largest single soundstage. The Sanderson cottage and Old Burial Hill graveyard were both built from scratch inside.

The crew imported region-specific dirt and wood to inspire the cast with an escapist and distinctively woodsy smell. All these years later, cast members still mention that smell in interviews. Thora Birch tells fans she finds herself catching whiffs of it in her memory to this day.

The Sanderson cottage was authentically constructed and fully functional. "It's a mortise and tenon old-style architecture, where the logs are split and seamed together," explains production designer William Sandell. He and his crew used heavy timber instead of box timber and "shaped the wood by axing, grinding, and sandblasting to add a patina of age. We imitated a watte and daub, which is a technique of mixing clay with chopped straw used originally by New Englanders in lieu of plaster to weatherize their houses."

Sandell thought about moving the house to a hillside somewhere after production wrapped, thinking he could use it as a sort of artist's retreat (or even live in it).

Birch says she spent some of her downtime on the set exploring the cottage, going through its drawers, etc.

The water wheel, too, was built from scratch and really worked.

Kirschner compared the level of detail on Stage 2 to that of Main Street at Disneyland. The sets are similarly captivating.

While many of the sets were built in Hollywood, some of *Hocus Pocus*'s most iconic scenes were filmed on location in Salem, Massachusetts and nearby Marblehead during the fall of 1992. As it happens, those scenes were shot during the 300th Anniversary of the Salem Witch Trials, and the city was engaged in grand-scale historical commemorations at the time.

The 1693 scenes were shot in Pioneer Village, an actual living history museum dedicated to seventeenth-century Salem. It is still open to the public today. For that matter, many of the Massachusetts filming locations are still standing, and "*Hocus Pocus* tours" remain popular there.

Several other scenes were filmed in Whittier, California. Locations there include the city's Central Park, a nearby residential area, and the Uptown YMCA.

The "I Put a Spell on You" scene was shot inside the famous ballroom at the Park Plaza Hotel in Los Angeles.

Though never credited, several other scenes were shot at the Warner Ranch in Burbank, California. After the witches burn in the furnace, Max, Dani, and Allison celebrate in front of the same fountain seen in the opening sequence for TV's "Friends."

Even more significantly, the house just behind Max in that scene is the *same* house used for the Burnham family residence in *American Beauty* (1999). So in *Hocus Pocus*, young Thora Birch is celebrating in front of the same home her *American Beauty* character would reside in six years later. (Incidentally, the house first appeared in yet another holiday classic. It is the Griswolds' brightly lit home in 1989's *National Lampoon's Christmas Vacation*.)

Music

The entire score was recorded in just five days.

John Debney composed the logo music for both Walt Disney Pictures and Touchstone Pictures during the late '80s and '90s. It is his jingle you hear as the castle appears at the beginning of *Hocus Pocus* (and most other Disney movies of that era).

Midler, Parker, and Najimy each provide their own singing voices in "I Put a Spell on You." Midler said the other two were so nervous about the prospect of recording with The Divine Miss M, they were literally shaking in the studio.

Swedish pop duo Roxette (best known for the hit song, "It Must Have Been Love") wrote and recorded a number for *Hocus Pocus's* end credits, but the filmmakers decided to reprise "I Put a Spell on You" and score cues instead. Not wanting it to go to waste, Disney stuck the song in *Super Mario Bros.* (1993), where it makes very little sense — the refrain still kicks off with "I love when you do that hocus pocus to me." (Then again, a poppy love ballad would have been an odd ending for *Hocus Pocus*.) Critics panned the song and it failed to gain much traction on the U.S. charts, but it became a Top Ten hit in the U.K. and throughout much of Europe.

Some Additional Observations from Your Author

When Winifred casts the black-flame candle spell, her book drops to the ground and its pages flip open rapidly. Advancing frame by frame, we find a variety of fully scripted and chillingly dark spells in the book (some of them repeated several times). Religious references, including the Hebrew names for God, are replete. The book even explains that, upon casting the black-flame spell, the witches' souls will abide in the hills around their house until released by a virgin on a full-moon Halloween night. That might help explain the witches' vague understanding of events that unfolded there prior to their return.

While Mrs. Olin teaches the class about the Sandersons, Max is doodling "The Grateful Dead" in his notebook. It's ostensibly a reference to the rock band, but we might also read it as foreshadowing. In literature, "grateful dead" is an archetypal folk tale in which a traveler stumbles upon a dead body that was never properly buried. When the traveler rights this wrong, the ghost appears to thank him for his good deed. (As a matter of fact, the rock band named themselves after the literary trope.) Later, Max helps Thackery lay his body to rest at long last. At the end of the movie, Thackery's ghost appears and thanks Max for setting him free, becoming a grateful dead.

Just above the Grateful Dead sketch, Max draws a peace sign and what appears to be a marijuana leaf.

Other than Max, the children in Mrs. Olin's class are all dressed in non-period-specific attire. This achieves two goals: emphasizing Max as an outsider in his new home and grounding the movie in a timeless aesthetic.

Instead of the portrait of President Clinton we find in most 1990s movie classrooms, the portraits on Mrs. Olin's walls are of olden Salem types. Here again, the effect is to lend a timeless quality to the production instead of rooting it so squarely in the 1990s.

Signs outside the cottage indicate the museum is part of the larger Salem Historical Park / Preservation, which also includes a "witch trail." I can't be the only one who wants to know what's down that path.

As the witches exit the bus, Winifred exclaims, "Odd's Bodkins!" It sounds like a nonsensical phrase today, but it has its roots in blasphemy. In Puritan times, "God's body" or "God's dear body" was used either as a solemn oath or as a kind of cuss word — the sort of thing one might say when stumping one's toe. To take the Lord's name in vain was an extremely serious offense, and so well-meaning potty mouths looked for a less offensive swear. A bodkin is a small tool used to punch holes in leather. People borrowed the word because it sounded like "body." And "Odd's" because it sounded like "God's." So "odd's bodkins" became a milder turn of phrase, though still considered rather profane. When Winifred uses it, she's being very PG by 1693 standards, if not PG-13. How appropriate.

The phrase "hocus pocus" might have similar origins. While some suspect they are only nonsense words with no real etymology to speak of, there is some evidence to suggest the phrase might have originated as a corruption of "hoc est corpus meum" (translated as "this is my body") in the Catholic liturgy of the Eucharist. Some even believe the famous hokey pokey began as a song-and-dance mockery of Catholicism, a play on the same "hocus pocus" riff. Scholars have been unable to make a clear and convincing case for any of the competing lineages.

The witches burning inside the furnace acts as a kind of parable for the burning of witches at the stake.

The name Thackery might have originated with *Hocus Pocus*, but it has turned up in literature, television, and film a number of times since (including in Disney and Tim Burton's *Alice in Wonderland* franchise).

The name is likely inspired by William Makepeace Thackeray, a nineteenth-century satirist, author, and illustrator. Among his many works is an 1859 novel, *The Virginians: A Tale of the Last Century*, about a Colonial village. In it, the characters attend a performance of *Macbeth*. Thackeray included his sketch of the play's three Weird Sisters in the text.

At one point, Winifred shouts out to Billy, yelling, "Hold onto your head!" Her intonation clearly echoes Disney's Queen of Hearts. The character was one of Midler's chief inspirations in creating Winnie.

Hocus Pocus isn't the only 1990s family film to use the phrase "firefly from Hell." Robin Williams's Peter Banning calls Tinker Bell the same thing when he first encounters her in *Hook* (1991).

Legacy

The movie grossed $39.5 million at the box office — a meager return, given the $28 million production budget.

While most of the reviews were unkind, there *were* a few positive assessments among them. Most notable was *The Hollywood Reporter*, which wrote, "Ortega's nimble narrative choreography propels [the story] along... always fast on its feet, in large part because of the hoary aplomb of Midler, Parker, and Najimy." The *Orlando Sentinel* also offered high praise, saying the movie is better than it has any right to be and going so far as to draw favorable comparisons between computer-animated Binx and the dinosaurs of *Jurassic Park*. And even the unflattering reviews tended to single out Thora Birch's performance as impressive. [27]

Disney Press published a novelization by Todd Strasser, now long out of print. Released in 1993, the novel carried an SRP of just $2.95 in the United States. Strasser's version includes several deviations from the film, including some of the deleted scenes and alternative storylines described above. The book includes thirteen full-color production stills.

The movie has been released to home video just three times: VHS in pan-and-scan (September 9, 1994), DVD in non-anamorphic widescreen (June 4, 2002), and finally Blu-ray in high definition (September 4, 2012). Both the DVD and Blu-ray are still in print from Walt Disney Home Entertainment, and the movie is also available for purchase as an HD digital download.

During the five-year period between 2007 and 2013 alone, *Hocus Pocus's* home video sales totaled $8,214,943, almost all of it in the October months.[28] That is an incredible sum for a catalogue title.

The October broadcasts on ABC Family (now Freeform) attract between 1 and 3 million viewers each time. In 2015, the network secured the rights to air the movie *ten times*, including two back-to-back broadcasts on Halloween night — the most the movie has ever been shown on the same channel in the same year. (2016's numbers were not available as this book went to press.) The network's director of acquisitions told *Yahoo! Movies*, "It's one of our highest-rated titles, consistently... it's really become kind of a foundation of the [13 Days of Halloween] event."[29] [30]

Since the time of Hocus Pocus's release in 1993, annual Halloween spending in the U.S. has grown from about $2.5 - 3 billion to $10 - 12 billion.

The movie earned five Saturn Award nominations (Best Actress for Midler, two in Best Supporting Actress for Parker and Najimy, Best Fantasy Film, Best Special Effects) and one win (Best Costumes).

Thora Birch won Best Youth Actress: Leading Role in a Motion Picture – Comedy at the Young Artist Awards that year (known then as the Youth in Film Awards) in a tie with Christina Vidal (*Life with Mikey*). Shaw was nominated in the same category.

Likewise, Katz and Murray were each nominated for Best Youth Actor: Leading Role in a Motion Picture – Comedy. Marsden, meanwhile, earned a nom for Best Youth Actor in a Voice-Over Role: TV or Movie. (Both Marsden and Murray were given unrelated nods for their work in other roles that year too.)

In many other countries, *Hocus Pocus* is called *Abracadabra*.

Hocus Pocus is an IMDb "Known For" credit for Midler, Najimy, and Ortega. (Parker's "Known For" field is dominated by *Ed Wood* and "Sex and the City.")

In 2011, the Houston Symphony staged a Halloween concert entitled *Hocus Pocus Pops*, featuring score selections from this and other Halloween-themed films. It was a hit. Let's hope the idea catches on in other cities.

In 2013, many members of the cast and crew assembled at the Disney Studios for a 20th Anniversary screening and retrospective panel. Even Omri Katz, largely retired from the entertainment industry, made an appearance.

In 2015, Midler performed "I Put a Spell on You" in full Winifred regalia as part of her sold-out *Divine Intervention* tour. The performance met mixed reviews — older audience members didn't understand it, while younger fans went nuts. It offered the evening's most theatrical moment. Through set pieces and projection technology, Midler recreated the Sanderson cottage on her stage, and her Harlettes dressed as Sarah and Mary. In addition to the song, she featured score from the film, told jokes as Winifred, and even recited bits of dialogue. The concert program included a two-page, full-color spread commemorating the movie.

"I'd be happy playing her for the rest of my life," Midler says of Winifred.

"Quite frankly," John Debney says of the movie, "it still is one of my best-sounding and best-played scores after these almost twenty years. *Hocus Pocus* is still one of my personal favorites. The energy in the room was palpable and the artistry of the performance is stellar."[31]

"Do you know that there are so many crazy *Hocus Pocus* fans out there?" Najimy asks. "It's insane. I knew it was kind of popular, but once Twitter came along, I'd say 90 percent of my followers, all they do is freak out all day long: 'When is there gonna be a sequel?' 'When is there gonna be a Broadway show?' 'Watching *Hocus Pocus*!' It's crazy."[32]

In recalling the first time she saw the movie, Shaw says, "I remember seeing the first shot over the water, and the music coming up. I grew up on Disney movies, and it just felt old school. Even the writing, the font, seems like you're expecting Julie Andrews to be a part of it."[33]

Disney's D23 fan club sums the film's legacy best, declaring the movie to have "attained near-mythic pop culture status."[34]

Watch This!

In addition to the many movies discussed at length throughout this book, *Hocus Pocus* fans might find the following titles enjoyable and/or illuminating:

The Halloween Tree (1993)

Four friends dress up for trick-or-treating, but they're alarmed when a fifth, Pip, is missing. Soon, they learn Pip is on the brink of death in the hospital, and his spirit has been whisked away on a journey that will determine his fate. With the help of a decrepit old man they meet in the woods (Leonard Nimoy), they manage to follow Pip's spirit through time, and along the way, they encounter the various traditions that made Halloween what it is today — the mummies of Egypt, the Day of the Dead in Mexico, All Souls' Night at Notre Dame, and a Celtic coven of witches.

Ray Bradbury first published *The Halloween Tree* as a novel in 1972. Hanna-Barbera debuted the full-length animated feature in October 1993, with a screenplay adapted by Bradbury himself, who also narrates. *Hocus Pocus*'s David Kirschner serves as executive producer and John Debney composes the score. This is Debney's only other Halloween soundtrack, released just months after *Hocus Pocus*, and its influence is apparent. Bradbury makes a Disney connection too. He was a close friend of Walt's and was instrumental in developing EPCOT Center and its Spaceship Earth.

Something Wicked This Way Comes (1983)

Bradbury self-adapted another of his novels in *Something Wicked This Way Comes*, a creepy fantasy set in an ominous 1930s autumn. A carnival is on its way to town, but right from the start, something seems not quite right. A tall and mysterious man named Mr. Dark (Jonathan Pryce) runs the show, and he's promising to fulfill the townspeople's deepest desires. He can deliver, but always at an unpleasant price. Our protagonists, two young boys named Will Halloway and Jim Nightshade, sense there's something sinister lurking within the carnival tents. So does Will's father, local librarian Charles Halloway (Jason Robards). A little research reveals this isn't the first time the carnival has come around, and things didn't go so well last time.

Like *Hocus Pocus*, *Something Wicked* was a brave endeavor for the studio. It is downright dark and incredibly atmospheric. Its PG rating notwithstanding, the movie is sure to disturb audiences of all ages.

Big Business (1988)

In an extremely high-concept premise (loosely based on Shakespeare's *Comedy of Errors*), a wealthy business owner and his wife give birth to identical twins on the same day and in the same hospital as a couple of poorly educated furniture makers they employ. An incompetent nurse accidentally switches two of the twins. Fast-forward a few decades, and Manhattan executives Sadie and Rose Shelton (Bette Midler and Lily Tomlin) are trying to offload the little furniture company they still own, incensing employees Sadie and Rose Ratliff (Bette Midler and Lily Tomlin).

While its wildly farcical plot won't be everyone's cup of tea, *Big Business* surely remains one of Midler's funniest films. You'll love it or hate it, and if you're in the former camp, you'll cry with laughter every time. It's nature vs. nurture, city mouse vs. country mouse, and Wall Street vs. Main Street rolled into one. While *Ruthless People* and *Down and Out in Beverly Hills* earned bigger box office receipts, *Big Business* better stands the test of time and might be the most durable of Midler's early Disney/Touchstone hits. Bette showcases two dramatically different performances in this *Parent Trap*-esque escapade, and Winifred is sometimes reminiscent of her haughty Sadie Shelton here.

Return to Oz (1985)

Set six months after *The Wonderful Wizard of Oz* and loosely inspired by several of L. Frank Baum's follow-ups, *Return to Oz* is one of the weirdest Disney movies ever made. It is exemplary of the studio's edgier, experimental filmmaking during the 1980s, which paved the way for *Hocus Pocus*. It is as fascinating as it is unusual.

George Lucas is to *Return to Oz* as Steven Spielberg is to *Hocus Pocus*. Lucas didn't produce or direct, and his only credit is a special thank you from the filmmakers, but he did spend time on the set. The crew is largely comprised of artists who worked with Lucas on Disney's *Captain EO*, and the two films bear a distinctively Lucas style. When budgets ballooned and production hit a snag, it was Lucas (along with Francis Ford Coppola, also involved in *EO*) who convinced Disney not to pull the plug. In the end, the final cut has the look and feel of a mid-80s Lucas blockbuster. And with a witch, a jack-o'-lantern, and a scarecrow in its cast of characters, the movie is even primed for Halloweentime viewing.

Halloweentown (1998)

Unexpectedly popular for a Disney Channel Original Movie, *Halloweentown* earned a reputation as *Hocus Pocus*'s little sister. It's a milder and less ambitious movie, but equally steeped in the festivity of fall.

Debbie Reynolds stars as Aggie Cromwell, a widely respected witch whose daughter has turned her back on their home, a parallel dimension called Halloweentown. But when Aggie's granddaughter starts to show signs of magic around her thirteenth birthday, Aggie sees an opportunity to bring her daughter back into the fold — and just in time to counter an inexplicable darkness creeping up in the citizens of Halloweentown.

"Eerie, Indiana" (1991)

Envisioned as a kind of "Twin Peaks" for kids, this TV Series chronicles the adventures of Marshall Teller (Omri Katz) in his new hometown of Eerie, IN, population of 16,661. Strange things happen here, and nearly every resident is bizarre. Among them is Dash X (Jason Marsden), a mysterious gray-haired kid who lives on the streets, eats out of dumpsters, and has no recollection of his parents or his past.

The show premiered on NBC and ran for one season (September 1991 – April 1992), but the network cancelled it before the final episode aired. The Disney Channel picked it up for syndication the next year, and began airing reruns (including the unaired finale) in 1993. Disney took it off the schedule in 1996, prompting Fox to pick up the reruns in '97. By then, the short-lived series had acquired a cult following, prompting a spin-off series, "Eerie, Indiana: The Other Dimension," at Fox in 1998.

The First Wives Club (1996)

When lonely housewife Cynthia (Stockard Channing) takes her own life, her three best friends from college are devastated. Life hasn't been so kind to them, either. Annie (Diane Keaton) is in marriage counseling, Elise (Goldie Hawn) is a washed-up actress and alcoholic with an ex-husband film producer threatening her career, and Brenda (Bette Midler) is in a financial struggle after her husband left her for a much younger woman named Shelly (Sarah Jessica Parker). Cynthia's death prompts them to reunite, reassess, and hatch a plot for revenge.

The satisfying and hilarious payback caper was Midler's first time on the big screen post-*Pocus*, and it's nearly as beloved today. There is perpetual talk of a sequel, and a Broadway musical is already in the works. The star-studded cast also includes Maggie Smith, Victor Garber, Stephen Collins, Marcia Gay Harden, Elizabeth Berkley, and Bronson Pinchot, with cameos by Kathie Lee Gifford, Gloria Steinem, Ed Koch, Ivanka Trump, Heather Locklear, and an early appearance by J.K. Simmons.

Mr. Boogedy (1986)

Whereas *Hocus Pocus* began as a TV movie that ended up in theaters, *Boogedy*'s trajectory was just the opposite. Producers whittled its feature-length script down to a 45-minute TV special, hosted by Michael Eisner on ABC's "The Disney Sunday Movie" in April 1986. (Here again, Disney picked an odd time of year for a Halloween-y release). It's the story of a gag gift salesman whose family moves into an old house in New England, only to discover Colonial ghosts are haunting it.

Corny but surprisingly spooky, the special made a lasting impact on children of the era. (The movie and its feature-length sequel, *Bride of Boogedy*, re-aired well into the '90s.) For many years, it ranked among the most frequently requested titles in Disney's out-of-print vault. Finally, in 2014, the company answered fan demand and made both *Boogedy* movies available for digital download. The Turner Classic Movies website describes *Mr. Boogedy* as a precursor to films like *Beetlejuice*, *The Addams Family*, and *Hocus Pocus*.

The Witches (1990)

Young orphan Luke vacations in England with his ailing grandmother, Helga. Their hotel just happens to host the Royal Society for the Prevention of Cruelty to Children, which Luke soon learns is actually a convention for child-killing witches in disguise. When the attendees catch Luke and turn him into a mouse, Helga must help him defeat the Grand High Witch (Anjelica Huston).

The Witches has the distinction of being the final film Jim Henson worked on before passing away, the final Roald Dahl film adaptation released during Dahl's lifetime, and the last movie from Lorimar Productions. It earned rave reviews but performed poorly at the box office. Nevertheless, it remains one of the more popular witch-themed family films from the '90s.

Online Resources

Find more *Hocus Pocus* fun and enlightenment with these helpful online resources. Note: the links below may contain adult language, and the content contained therein may change subsequent to publication.

The Three CommentEARS: Episode 10 – "Hocus Pocus"
Film gurus Albert Gutierrez, Kelvin Cedeño, and Pedro Hernandez are your hosts for this unofficial, fan-made audio commentary. Follow the easy instructions to line up their audio track with your DVD or Blu-ray. *bit.ly/2aSwWo9*

Hocus Broke-Us
The Disney fan community is lucky to have Todrick Hall, the multi-talented YouTube entertainer with an affinity for Mouse-inspired productions. His hilarious parody of the film recasts Winifred as Seyoncé (Hall), with the tagline "Halloween has never been so ratchet." *bit.ly/1jBUX7q*

Evolution of Disney
Todrick Hall takes us through the musical history of Disney in this impressive medley, which includes a pit stop in 1993 for "I Put a Spell on You." *bit.ly/1H437xM*

Hocus Pocus Parody by The Hillywood Show®

The "Sanderson sisters" perform a clever and impressively produced parody of "Kidnap the Sandy Claws" from *The Nightmare Before Christmas*. *bit.ly/1lr8mda*

Hocus Pocus Re-Review – Disneycember 2015

When the web's Nostalgia Critic first encountered *Hocus Pocus*, he was, by his own admission, pretty harsh. But in this re-review (the first he's ever done), the N.C. begins to reassess. While he's still not quite a convert, any fan of the movie will be heartened to hear his evolving observations. *bit.ly/2aSywpR*

Nostalgia Chick 10/31/08 - Hocus Pocus

The Nostalgia Chick treats the movies to her dry-humored wit. *bit.ly/2aUUITm*

Discovery Channel's "Movie Magic"

In the 1990s, the Discovery Channel aired "Movie Magic," a documentary series about the art and science of moviemaking. Several of the episodes go behind the scenes on the set of *Hocus Pocus*. While the show has never been released on home video, the relevant episodes are (as of this printing) preserved on YouTube.

> *Episode 1*: "Creature Makeup: Masks and Mirrors" (1994, includes several sequences with Doug Jones and Billy Butcherson) *bit.ly/2aUxH5J*

> *Episode 9*: "Computer Animation: Electric Dreams" (1994, offers an in-depth look at the creation of Thackery Binx, not to mention interviews with a very young John Lasseter) *bit.ly/2bi8aOW*

> *Episode 10:* "Cinematic Flight: Up, Up and Away" (1994, nearly the entire episode is devoted to the flight effects in *Hocus Pocus*) *bit.ly/2cawoht*

"Come Little Children" (katethegreat19 cover)
Under stage name Erutan, YouTuber katethegreat19 offers a fresh arrangement of Sarah Jessica Parker's song, earning over a million views.
bit.ly/2b9okK3

"Come Little Children" (Traci Hines cover)
Disney fan and YouTube songstress TraciJHines puts her viral twist on Sarah's song.
bit.ly/2aUzese

"I Put a Spell on You" (Traci Hines cover, featuring Lauren Matesic)
Hines, Matesic, and special guest Chrissy Lynn certainly look the part as Sarah, Winifred, and Mary, respectively. In a subtle plot twist, Sarah ends up singing the bulk of Winifred's lines.
bit.ly/1XlrbC7

Hocus Pocus Spellbook Cookies
Nerdy Nummies star Rosanna Pansino invites special guest Jen Chae to join her in this do-it-yourself tutorial for baking cookies inspired by Winifred's spell book.
bit.ly/2aMtFe8

Excerpts from a 1996 Disney Channel Halloween marathon
Still need more nostalgia? Have a blast from the past with this *Hocus Pocus*-centric reel of Disney Channel interstitial programming.
bit.ly/2br5PCY

"From Bette Midler to Beth Leavel: Dream Casting a *Hocus Pocus* Musical"
Playbill imagines a full-scale Broadway adaptation and ponders who would play whom.
bit.ly/2br6HqT

"Sing, Sisters! Here's How We Think *Hocus Pocus* Should Be Imagined for the Stage (With Song Titles and Sorcery)"
Still not satisfied, *Playbill* taps composer-lyricist Joey Contreras to develop a potential song list — all originals, mind you — for their hypothetical

Broadway show. (That makes two *Playbill* articles on the topic, Disney! Let's make this happen!)
bit.ly/2b4xaeW

DizRadio

The folks at DizRadio.com, an unofficial Disney fan podcast and website, are huge *Hocus Pocus* fans. They've invited cast members on for one interview after another, including:

> *Episode #52*: Thora Birch *bit.ly/2cp1h2u*
> *Episode #89*: Tobias Jelinek *bit.ly/2bKTllD*
> *Episode #122*: Thora Birch *bit.ly/2cnTdMu*

Bootleg Betty

The world's biggest Bette Midler fansite and blog.
www.bootlegbetty.com

Notes

Introduction

1. "Hocus Pocus." *Rotten Tomatoes*, Web. 1 July 2016. <bit.ly/2bpqxWx>.
2. Abad-Santos, Alex. "Hocus Pocus is a garbage movie that doesn't deserve your nostalgia." *Vox*, 30 Oct. 2015. Web. 31 July 2016. <bit.ly/1GPUpEZ>.
3. "Auteur." *Oxford Dictionaries*. Oxford University Press, Web. 1 July 2016. <bit.ly/2aA3JOL>.
4. Lehman, Peter, and William Luhr. *Thinking About Movies: Watching, Questioning, Enjoying*. 2nd ed. Blackwell Publishing, 2003 : p. 381. Print.

Chapter 1 - The Home Alone of Halloween

1. EW Staff. "Which Pop Culture Witch Are You?" *Entertainment Weekly*, 28 Oct. 2015. Web. 31 Jul. 2016. <bit.ly/2aS8fgP>.
2. We will return to Mickey's Not-So-Scary Halloween Party in *Chapter Eleven*. For more on the 2015 event's sales, see: Chaney, Jen. "The Magical Tale of How 'Hocus Pocus' Went From Box-Office Flop to Halloween Favorite." *Yahoo! Movies*, 28 Oct. 2015. Web. 31 July 2016. <yhoo.it/1ReihTh>.
3. See this book's *Epilogue*.
4. In a 2013 appearance on "Katie," Midler told Ms. Couric, "We made [*Hocus Pocus*] before the tidal wave of Halloween happened. You know, I mean, in the old days, Halloween was… 'Oh, it's Halloween… the kids will go out'… but now it's, like, *huge*; it's huge.

The kids, grownups, everybody takes part in it, and this movie was kind of... at the beginning of the wave." Looking back, *Hocus Pocus* might have helped start that wave. Prior to 1993, surprisingly few theatrically released films had been explicitly set during the Halloween season, and fewer still either made the holiday a focal point or found significant success. A handful of slasher movies did, however, make Halloween their home (most prominent among them is 1978's *Halloween*), and notable entries in the family Halloween genre came in 1982 with *E.T. the Extra-Terrestrial* and in 1991 with Touchstone's *Ernest Scared Stupid*. The generation responsible for adding billions to the Halloween industry's GDP is the same that brought *Hocus Pocus* back from the deep.

5. Chaney, Note 2, above.

6. Bieber's remarks came in response to a *very* sharp and saucy joke Midler had tweeted after one of the young star's photo scandals. (Martins, Chris. "Billboard Cover: Justin Bieber Says 'I Was Close to Letting Fame Destroy Me.'" *Billboard*, 5 Nov. 2015. Web. 31 Jul. 2016. <bit.ly/1NuwWKQ>.) Taking his jab in stride, Midler tweeted back at Bieber, saying, "Britt Medler! I don't know who that is either! But damn that bitch!" 5 Nov. 2015, 3:25 p.m. Tweet. <bit.ly/2aS8N6n>.

7. Each of these stories can be likened to "The Hero's Journey" (sometimes called "The Monomyth"), a common narrative template in which a hero goes on an adventure; faces incredible challenges, temptations, or crises of character; and then returns home as a changed or transformed person. The "Journey" often takes the form a three-act narrative. Several critics have written about Max's story in *Hocus Pocus* as a mythical "Hero's Journey," and sure enough, the movie is an effective model of a protagonist's adventure unfolding in three taught acts. The original Christmas story (Jesus Christ's birth) might also be read as a Hero's Journey. In turn, that might explain why The Monomyth is so prevalent in holiday stories. For that matter, as "the greatest story ever told," the Nativity tale might account for the prevalence of the Hero's Journey in pop culture, generally. For more on the Bible as a prototype for The Monomyth, see: Merritt, Jonathan. "The Greatest Story Ever Told?" *The Atlantic*, 24 Dec. 2015. Web. 31 Jul. 2015. <theatln.tc/1Pmy30g>.

8. Perhaps it is no coincidence Max and Allison attend Jacob Bailey High School. The name immediately calls to mind two of the most famous Christmas characters: Jacob Marley of *A Christmas Carol* and George Bailey of *It's a Wonderful Life*. Alternatively, the name might be in reference to: Rev. Jacob Bailey (1731 – 1808, an American writer who fled to Canada, fearing persecution for his Loyalist sentiments and his position as a

clergyman in the Church of England), Jacob Bailey Moore (1797 – 1853, an American journalist and historian), or Jacob Whitman Bailey (1811 – 1857, a Massachusetts-born scientist).

Chapter 2 - Make Halloween Great Again: Jurassic Park, Nostalgia, and the Seven Gables of Salem

1. While the mansion is best known as The House of the Seven Gables, it is believed to have had as few as three and as many as eight gables over the years.

2. As the story goes, while working as a pastor, Horace Conolly (the adopted son of Susannah Ingersoll) heard an interesting story about a young Acadian girl searching for her long lost love. He shared the story with Nathaniel Hawthorne and encouraged him to fictionalize it. Hawthorne said he would, but after several years passed, Conolly grew impatient and gave the story to Henry Wadsworth Longfellow, who immediately adapted it as a poem, "Evangeline, A Tale of Acadie." Hawthorne supposedly grew resentful, insisting Conolly had given Longfellow a more interesting version of the tale, though the two ultimately returned to good terms. Some have challenged the veracity of that account, contending Hawthorne gave it to Longfellow himself. At any rate, many years later, the same poem would inspire the characters Ray and Evangeline in *The Princess and the Frog*. As we will see later, this is the first of several intriguing connections between Disney's 2009 animated feature and *Hocus Pocus*.

3. For more on the history of The House of the Seven Gables, see "The House of the Seven Gables (The Turner-Ingersoll Mansion)." *The House of the Seven Gables*, Web. 24 July 2016. <bit.ly/2aUSORy>.

4. William Sandell (born 1950), sometimes credited as Bill Sandell (including in *Hocus Pocus*), is an American art director of Hollywood motion pictures. He got his start by working on "B-movies" during the 1970s, with an early break as an uncredited set dresser on Scorsese's *Mean Streets* (1973). His later production design credits include *RoboCop* (1987), Midler's *Big Business* (1988), *Total Recall* (1990), *Nothing But Trouble* (1991), Ortega's *Newsies* (1992), *The Flintstones* (1994), *Air Force One* (1997), and *The Perfect Storm* (2000). He received an Oscar nomination for his work on *Master and Commander: The Far Side of the World* (2003).

5. It wasn't the only influence. Sandell and his team wanted the house to have a gothic feel but with a fantastical quality, not unlike the cottage we might imagine for Hansel and Gretel's witch in the woods (*sans* candy). We can find influences ranging from Salem's

Pioneer Village (where some of the early shots were actually filmed) to *The Wizard of Oz* (in the image on Page 34, notice that the tree branch just above the cottage's rightmost gable takes the shape of a hand, calling to mind both the apple-throwing trees and the Haunted Forest of Oz).

6. That's Allison's explanation, but the sign outside the cottage says "Closed for Renovations." Did the museum's operators really intend to reopen it?

7. *Jurassic World* (2015) is the fourth theatrical release in the *Jurassic Park* film franchise, following the original *Jurassic Park* (1993), *The Lost World: Jurassic Park* (1997), and *Jurassic Park III* (2001). All four films are available on home video from Universal Pictures Home Entertainment. A fifth film is reportedly slated for release in 2018.

8. Urban decay photographer Seph Lawless (born 1978) emphasizes commercial spaces. See *SephLawless.com* for more.

Chapter 3 - Spielberg's Second-Best Halloween Movie

1. Steven Spielberg (born 1946) is an American film director, generally considered one of the greatest, most pioneering, and most successful directors in Hollywood history. Among his many notable credits are *E.T. the Extra-Terrestrial* (1982), *The Color Purple* (1985), *Hook* (1991), *Jurassic Park* (1993), *Schindler's List* (1993), *Saving Private Ryan* (1988), and *Minority Report* (2002). He is also well known as an executive producer of sci-fi, fantasy, action-adventure, and thriller films.

2. If *Hocus Pocus* is any *one* person's movie, it's Bette Midler's. Relatively few performers achieve the status of the "actor-auteur," stars who burn so brightly their movies are different simply because they're in them. These are "actors whose strong personalities can inform the mood, pacing, and structure of an entire film." (Levy, Emanuel. "John Wayne: Star as Auteur." *Emanuel Levy: Cinema 24/7*, 13 April 2011. Web. 14 July 2016. <bit.ly/2aFqSje>.) To become one, an actor needs a certain amount of leverage within Hollywood: the power to pick their own projects or to otherwise sculpt films in their individual artistic styles. Auteurism in acting is more than just typecasting or a box office bonanza; it is the wielding of creative influence, such that a study of an individual film in light of the actor's personal life and broader body of work becomes illuminating. John Wayne, James Cagney, Johnny Depp, and Mae West are cited the most. Bette Midler probably belongs among them. We can learn more about *Hocus Pocus* because she's in it, and in turn, the movie teaches us about its star too. The fact that it has musical sequences, that it is edgier than most Disney movies, that it is larger than life and

overflowing with camp — these qualities make it a Bette Midler movie, and it might not have had them without her. We will look more closely at Midler's impact on the movie and the character in *Chapter Four*.

3. See *Introduction*, Note 3.

4. *This Is It* (2009) came to theaters as a concert documentary, directed by Kenny Ortega, in the wake of Michael Jackson's death. The film captures Jackson's final days, as he rehearses for an ill-fated series of concerts entitled *This Is It*. Ortega appears as himself throughout the film, working closely with Jackson on a number of performances, including "Thriller." In the film, Jackson's iconic Halloween-themed song is presented as both a live performance a brand-new music video short film, inspired by Disney's Haunted Mansion attractions.

5. Gene Kelly (1912 – 1996) was an American actor, dancer, singer, director, producer, and choreographer. He is widely considered one of the greatest dancers of the Hollywood era. He is best known for his roles in *An American in Paris* (1951) and *Singin' in the Rain* (1952). He also directed *Hello, Dolly!*, starring Barbra Streisand, in 1969. Kelly's final film role was in *Xanadu* (1980), starring alongside Olivia Newton-John.

6. In addition to Kenny Ortega, *Hocus Pocus* and St. *Elmo's Fire* (1985) also share William Sandell among their credits. He was the production designer for both films.

7. Unquestionably, so many other people had an indispensable hand in giving *Hocus Pocus* the aesthetic presence it has today: story creators Kirschner and Garris (see Notes 10 and 11 below), production designer Sandell (see *Chapter Two*, Note 4), costume designer Mary Vogt, composer John Debney (see *Chapter Six*), and the list goes on.

8. In Hollywood's earlier days, individual studio styles were much easier to delineate. One of the best examples is the MGM musical, which audiences understood to be different from, say, a Twentieth Century-Fox musical. But as the old-school studio system fell by the wayside and as the industry has evolved, the idea of the "major studio as genre" is barely identifiable outside of Disney today.

9. As for intertextuality, consider this: the witches encounter a child dressed as Mrs. Potts from *Beauty and the Beast* — the closest Bette Midler and Angela Lansbury have ever come as co-stars. We will look more closely at intertextuality in *Chapter Five*.

10. David Kirschner (born 1955) is an American story developer, artist, and film and television producer, best known for his work in animation. He got his start as an illustrator for musician Neil Diamond's album covers. Later, he provided artwork for Jim Henson's "Sesame Street" and The Muppets, before moving on to a career in film.

His credits include *An American Tail* (1986), *Child's Play* (1988), *Hocus Pocus* (1993), *The Halloween Tree* (1993), and *The Pagemaster* (1994).

11. Mick Garris (born 1951) is an American screenwriter and director, best known for his work in sci-fi and horror. His credits include **batteries not included* (1987), *The Fly II* (1989), *Psycho IV: The Beginning* (1990), and *Hocus Pocus* (1993). He is well known for his work on television series "Amazing Stories" (with Steven Spielberg) and "Masters of Horror" (for Showtime). Garris also sits on the board of advisors for the Hollywood Horror Museum. For more, see this book's *Afterword*.

12. Greiving, Tim. Liner notes (print). *Hocus Pocus: Intrada Special Collection*. Intrada Records, 2013 : p. 4. CD.

13. This was not the first time Spielberg spent time on the set of a movie meant for him but made (officially) without him. *Poltergeist* (1982) came to theaters under the direction of Tobe Hooper, but critics have long suspected (and many crew members have reported) Spielberg was in fact the principal director. Those who've seen it can attest: it surely has the look and feel of a Spielberg feature! But the situation there isn't quite analogous to ours. Unlike with *Hocus Pocus*, Spielberg was credited as writer and producer on *Poltergeist*, and there is a plausible explanation for his stealthily directing it — his *E.T.* contract prevented him from helming *Poltergeist*. That's not quite the case with *Hocus Pocus*, and to be clear: nobody's arguing Spielberg secretly directed *Hocus Pocus*. Rather, it's that the movie was very much made in his style, whether purposely or not, that is interesting.

14. Greiving (see Note 12 above) first described *Hocus Pocus* as "sprinkled with Spielberg dust."

15. Is *Hocus Pocus* "Hitchcockian"? Probably not. While we do find a few common elements of The Master of Suspense — incompetent police officers, famous landmarks, pushing the envelope, regular people in extraordinary situations, a cool-headed blonde — critics usually look for bigger themes, like accusations against an innocent man, duplicity, MacGuffin plot devices, shocking climactic twists, intense suspense, the use of setting or shadow to create a sense of tension or danger, etc. While we might find traces of those elements in *Hocus Pocus*, there probably isn't a strong case for calling it "Hitchcockian" *per se*. We will consider, however, that the film could have been influenced in part by Hitchcock in *Chapters Seven* and *Eight*.

16. Film historians generally credit Spielberg and George Lucas with creating the blockbuster genre and regard *Jaws* (1975), *Star Wars* (1977), *Close Encounters of the Third Kind*

(1977), *Indiana Jones and the Raiders of the Lost Ark* (1981), and *E.T. the Extra-Terrestrial* (1982) as pivotal.

17. Not that Spielberg can't make bad movies, nor that reviewers have always loved him. During the '80s and '90s, in fact, many dismissed his films as sentimental elitism, decrying an apparent Peter Pan complex. (That particular chide lent some delicious irony to *Hook* in 1991. Even more ironically, the same critics who wished he would grow up back then tend to lament that *Munich*-era Spielberg has "lost touch" with his inner child now. But I digress.) They *did* pay attention, however. Rightly or wrongly, Spielberg films have unquestionably been better regarded on the whole than *Hocus Pocus* was upon release.

Chapter 4 - The Divine Miss Sanderson

1. "Do You Want to Dance" is the first track on Midler's debut album, *The Divine Miss M* (1972). She popularized her version with a steamy performance in her first television special, 1977's *Ol' Red Hair Is Back* (a play on Sinatra's *Old Blue Eyes Is Back*), winning a Primetime Emmy for Outstanding Variety, Music, or Comedy Special.

2. Best Actress in a Motion Picture Musical or Comedy (1979). To date, it is Midler's first of two wins in that specific category (the other came with 1990's *For the Boys*). She has a total of five nominations in the category (tied with Audrey Hepburn and Renee Zellweger). Only five other women have received more nominations in the same: Goldie Hawn and Barbra Streisand (seven), Julie Andrews (eight), and Meryl Streep and Shirley MacLaine (nine). Notably, this is the same category in which her *Hocus Pocus* costar, Thora Birch, would be nominated for *Ghost World* in 2001.

3. A few family-friendlier titles were scattered throughout, too: Touchstone-branded *Big Business* (PG, 1988); Disney-branded *Oliver & Company* (G, 1988); and *The Lottery* (1989), an unrated theme park short for the Disney-MGM Studios theme park in Walt Disney World.

4. "Bette Midler — Are You Surprised You Found a Home at Disney?" *Bootleg Betty*, 27 Aug. 2016. Web. <bit.ly/2bu9n55>.

5. So many of the performances in *Hocus Pocus* are strong. Kathy Najimy and Sarah Jessica Parker are uproarious. Omri Katz and Vinessa Shaw command the screen with the right blend of innocence and swagger, as though they'd each been playing the part of "Hollywood heartthrobs" for years (they hadn't). Jason Marsden finds the dignified side of sass in Thackery's voice. Thora Birch is funny, organic, endearing, and remarkably

never cloying. It's no wonder Ortega called her one of the top five actresses in her age group at the time, and the *Orlando Sentinel*'s 1993 review singled her out as "the Jodie Foster of a new generation" (prophetic, perhaps, given her Best Actress nomination at the Golden Globes years later).

6. With *It's the Girls!*, Midler became only the second woman in history (following Barbra Streisand) to chart a *Billboard* Top Ten album in each of the last five decades.

7. When Midler inked her big deal with Disney in the '80s, it allowed her to set up a production house of her very own within their walls. She called it All Girl Productions. The name was no accident, a simultaneous jab at Hollywood's "boys' club" and a wink at her onstage persona.

8. Midler made these comments during a 2006 appearance on "Late Show with David Letterman."

9. Margaret Dumont (1882 – 1965) was best known as the sidekick and comic foil in a number of Marx Brothers movies, earning her a reputation as "the fifth Marx Brother." While I have never known Midler to specifically credit Margaret Dumont as an influence, she did confirm Disney's Cruella and Queen of Hearts as bases for her performance in a press packet circulated at the time of release.

10. Azzopardi, Chris. "Divine Intervention: Bette Midler Talks Early Gay Support, 'Diva' Degradation & Twerking ('Girls, Please!')." *Pride Source*. Pride Source Media Group, LLC, 13 Nov. 2014. Web. 14 July 2016. <bit.ly/2ao2qIR>.

Chapter 5 - Everything's Coming Up Winnie: The Why of Her Whammy in "I Put a Spell on You"

1. Incidentally, she's even done a "witch song." Midler's self-titled second album (1973) opened Side B with a medley of "Lullaby of Broadway" and "Optimistic Voices." The latter originated in *The Wizard of Oz* (1939) (the eponymous voices sing as Glinda the Good Witch awakens Dorothy and her friends in a poppy field).

2. Conrich, Ian, and Estella Tincknell, editors. *Film's Musical Moments*. Edinburgh University Press Ltd, 2006 : pp. 1-2. Print.

3. "Backstage musicals" blur the line. In a backstage musical, characters are on-stage performers who are "supposed to be" singing. In those cases, the characters' achievement might simply be that they are doing their jobs.

4. Stephen Sondheim (born 1930) is an American playwright, composer, and lyricist whose contributions to musical theatre are widely considered to be some of the greatest among

living artists. His major works include *A Funny Thing Happened on the Way to the Forum*, *Company*, *Follies*, *A Little Night Music*, *Sweeney Todd: The Demon Barber of Fleet Street*, *Sunday in the Park with George*, and *Into the Woods*. He also wrote the lyrics for *Gypsy* and *West Side Story*. He's earned eight Tonys (including a Lifetime Achievement award), eight Grammys, an Oscar, and a Pulitzer Prize in Drama.

5. Ethel Merman originated the role of Rose on Broadway in 1959. In the original cast recording from that show, Merman says, "My name's Rose." Many subsequent versions, however, including Midler's own, drop the contraction, opting for "My name is Rose" instead. Rose's greeting is itself a callback to an earlier line in the musical by Rose's daughter, June. Such callbacks are common in Sondheim's work.

6. There seems to be a consensus among *Gypsy* enthusiasts that Midler's version is the definitive filming, and reviews at the time — including a downright glowing one from the *New York Times* — support that notion. It also directly paved the path for Disney's 1997 television adaptation of Rogers & Hammerstein's *Cinderella*, which became a huge hit of its own. (Whitney Houston reportedly phoned ABC and made arrangements to produce the special immediately after watching *Gypsy*.) The *Cinderella* cast features Broadway veteran Bernadette Peters, who would later star as Rose in a Broadway revival of *Gypsy*.

7. Because "I Put a Spell on You" is heard three times in the movie (first by Joseph Malone in the skeleton band, then by Midler, and again over the end credits), we might think of Midler's two performances as musical reprises.

8. "Vogue" is a 1990 dance-pop single by legendary pop artist Madonna. Fusing elements of disco and house music, the song became one of the biggest of the decade, selling six million copies and emerging as the most successful single of 1990. Visionary director David Fincher shot the accompanying music video in black-and-white, and "voguing" (Madonna's highly stylized choreography, imitated by Stephanie Faracy in *Hocus Pocus*) became synonymous with Madonna and early '90s pop. In 1999, MTV named the music video the second best of all time. The Rock and Roll Hall of Fame named it one of the "500 Songs That Shaped Rock and Roll" (along with "I Put a Spell on You").

9. Muir, John Kenneth. *Singing a New Tune: The Rebirth of the Modern Film Musical, from Evita to De-Lovely and Beyond*. Applause Theatre & Cinema Books, 2005 : pp. 81-85. Print.

Chapter 6 - Gardeners of Magic: James Horner, John Debney, and Sarah Jessica Parker

1. A clapper boy (sometimes called a clapper loader or, more modernly, the second assistant camera) is the member of a film crew responsible for loading camera magazines, working the clapperboard, and holding the slate up to the camera at the beginning of each take. The clapper boy (who may, of course, be female) is sometimes responsible for helping actors find their marks and might also be assigned a whole host of important logistical duties on the set.

2. Greiving, Tim. Liner notes (print). *Hocus Pocus: Intrada Special Collection*. Intrada Records, 2013 : p. 12. CD.

3. In making the observation, I don't mean to contend these are intentional references or that Debney was directly inspired by them.

4. The soundtrack is Volume #254 in Intrada Records' excellent Special Collection series. Mozart makes the cut, but the CD does not include "Sabre Dance" or "I Put a Spell on You" (the latter isn't part of Debney's library, and sadly, Disney has never released it in any official capacity). In issuing the score, which Intrada calls "both involved and complex," label executive Douglass Fake noted: "The Walt Disney production crew captured the score on then state-of-the-art 48-track digital recorders with veteran recording engineer John Richards in the booth. The result was a crisply played-and-recorded work full of technical craft and musical wizardry. To present this world premiere release of the score, Intrada was given access to the original 48-track digital scoring session elements vaulted at the Disney studios. Besides the appropriate instrumental positions of the various sections of the orchestra on the various tracks, engineer Richards had assigned an additional three separate tracks for the variety of percussion colors, another three tracks for the room ambience and three more tracks for the all-female chorus. The final spread of our newly-created two-track digital mix offers every instrumental and choral detail in dynamic sound." Fake also notes the "Intrada Special Collection release [is] available while quantities and interest remain!" so eager fans, take note! Fake, Douglass. "Hocus Pocus: Doug's Tech Talk." *Store.Intrada.com*. Intrada Records, Web. 18 July 2016. <bit.ly/2b7WsqG>.

5. The title isn't the only thing that causes confusion. The lyrics do too. In the film, Sarah sings four lines (and then repeats those same four lines), all of them written by Brock Walsh. That's all we hear on the Intrada soundtrack too. Over the years, though, addi-

tional verses have cropped up online, and no one knows where they came from. For a long time, popular consensus held that they were Edgar Allen Poe's. When Poe enthusiasts began to debunk that theory, horror writer and fellow Poe fan D. Melhoff decided to get to the bottom of the matter. His long quest for the truth led him first to Debney, then to Disney, then to Walsh, who insisted Poe did *not* write the original lyrics but that Walsh wasn't responsible for the web's new ones either. Hmmm. Still confused, Melhoff hired a licensing company to search out the source. Here's what they came back with:

Garden of Magic

from HOCUS POCUS*:

Text based on the poem "Come Little Children" by Edgar Allen Poe. Additional text by Brock Walsh.

Music by James Horner

(c) 1993 Walt Disney Music Company...

*Adapted lyrics not used in film...

Well, that can't be right. There is no historical evidence for a Poe(m) called "Come Little Children," and the "additional text" clearly isn't by Walsh. So what gives? Well, I suppose siren songs are *supposed* to be disorienting. For more, see: Melhoff, D. "Come Little Children." *DMelhoff.com*, Web. 18 July 2016. <bit.ly/2aTsrND>.

Chapter 7 - The Brave Little Virgin

1. For more, see: Mikkelson, David. "Disney Films: Urban legends and myths about Disney films." *Snopes.com*, Web. 24 June 2016. <bit.ly/2aA93Ex>.

2. For more on the *Back to the Future* theory, see: "BACK TO THE FUTURE predicts 9/11." *YouTube*, uploaded by barelyHuman11, 27 July 2015. Web. <bit.ly/1hvr86u>. For more on the Pixar theory, see *The Pixar Theory*. Web. 25 June 2016. <www.pixartheory.com>. See also: Negroni, Jon. "The Pixar Theory." *Jon Negroni Film Reviews*, 11 July 2013. Web. 25 June 2016. <bit.ly/2aS40px>. Both theories rely on some truly fascinating and apparently original observations, but in my estimation, their conclusions exceed the evidence.

3. Cavell, Stanley. *Pursuits of Happiness: The Hollywood Comedy of Remarriage*. Harvard University Press, 1981 : pp. 116-117. Print. See also: Deleyto, Celestino. "The New Road to Sexual Ecstacy: Virginity and Genre in *The 40 Year-Old Virgin*." *Virgin Territory: Representing Sexual Inexperience in Film*, edited by Tamar Jeffers McDonald, Wayne State University Press, 2010, pp. 255-256. Print.

4.   Alternatively, even if we were to concede that some audience members are not at all aware of what "virgin" means, those viewers will still understand, through context, that this mysterious word is of some great importance to the characters (and that an attitude of surprise or derision surrounds it).

5.   Mary's frequently on-the-fritz nasal abilities elude a clear reading. Because we can never trust whether she is actually smelling children (she often expresses uncertainty herself), her suspicions of nearby children might not point to much about what "child" really means. Alternatively, it is possible that while the sisters need virginal life force to survive, Mary's power of detection is limited to literal children (consistent with child-smelling villains in children's fiction, like the child catcher in *Chitty Chitty Bang Bang*) — a useful but imperfect skill.

6.   Even Vinessa Shaw has commented on the exchange. When asked at a press event whether the scene implies Allison is not a virgin, Shaw coyly replied with, "That is left to the imagination. A woman never reveals her cards!" Calderon, Arielle. "Allison from 'Hocus Pocus' Reveals Her Opinion On The Black Flame Candle Scene." *BuzzFeed*, 23 Sep. 2013. Web. 28 July 2016. <bzfd.it/2cdK7m3>.

7.   The Motion Picture Production Code (commonly referred to as the "Production Code" or simply "The Code") was a set of moral guidelines, practices, and standards applied to almost every movie produced by a major film studio in its era. A private organization, The Motion Picture Producers and Distributors of America (MPPDA), was responsible for enforcement. The MPPDA officially adopted the Code in 1930 and began concerted enforcement efforts in 1934. The Code came to be associated with two key figures: Will H. Hays (MPPDA president from 1922 to 1945, having assumed the position after his stints as U.S. Postmaster General and chairman of the Republican National Committee) and Joseph Breen (the administrator in charge of Code enforcement from 1934 to 1954, appointed by Hays). Because of their involvement, the Code is frequently referred to as "the Hays Code" or, less commonly, "the Breen Code." Hollywood steadfastly adhered to the Code throughout the '30s and '40s, but by the '50s, filmmakers and studios grew increasingly bold, spurred in part by the emerging competition from television. The story of the Code's decline is a long and complicated one, but in 1968, it was formally replaced by today's much less restrictive MPAA film rating system.

8.   Alfred Hitchcock (1899 – 1980) was an English film director, producer, and television personality, popularly known as "The Master of Suspense." Renowned as a pioneer in filmmaking and one of the greatest directors of all time, his earliest successes came

in British silent cinema. But it was his Hollywood feature work that would define his career, especially *Dial M for Murder* (1954), *Rear Window* (1954), *Vertigo* (1958), *North by Northwest* (1959), *Psycho* (1960), and *The Birds* (1963). On television, he hosted "Alfred Hitchcock Presents." For more on Hitchcock in the context of *Hocus Pocus*, see *Chapter Three*, Note 15.

9. Billy Wilder (1906 – 2002) was an Austrian-American screenwriter, film producer, and director, responsible for some of the most universally admired movies of his time. Among them: *Double Indemnity* (1944), *Sunset Boulevard* (1950), *Sabrina* (1954), *The Seven Year Itch* (1955), *Some Like It Hot* (1959), and *The Apartment* (1960). Wilder films are known for tight writing, smart dialogue, intriguing stories, and envelope-pushing subject matter (a contrast from his conservative cinematography).

10. Ebert, Roger. "Double Indemnity." *RogerEbert.com*, 20 Dec. 1998. Web. 24 June 2016. <bit.ly/2bkEh4P>.

11. An earlier version of the *Hocus Pocus* story, in which the Sandersons lured children to their cottage with magical candy, would have produced a wildly different reading. It probably would have made for a far less interesting movie too. For more, see the section on Alternate and Deleted Scenes within this book's *Bonus Material*.

12. See: McDonald, Tamar Jeffers. *Virgin Territory: Representing Sexual Inexperience in Film*. Wayne State University Press, 2010 : p. 9. Print.

Chapter 8 - Is Hocus Pocus a Horror Film?

1. Worland, Rick. *The Horror Film: An Introduction*. Blackwell Publishing, 2007 : pp. 9, 12. Print.

2. Worland 8-10, 12-15.

3. For a general discussion, see: Rockoff, Adam. *Going to Pieces: The Rise and Fall of the Slasher Film, 1978-1986*. McFarland & Company, Inc., 2002. See also: Kelly, Casey Ryan. *Abstinence Cinema: Virginity and the Rhetoric of Sexual Purity in Contemporary Film*. Rutgers University Press, 2016.

4. Royer, Carl, and Diana Royer, *The Spectacle of Isolation in Horror Films: Dark Parades*. The Haworth Press, 2005. Print.

5. Worland 8-9.

6. Carroll, Noël. *The Philosophy of Horror or Paradoxes of the Heart*. Routledge, 1990 : p. 16. Print.

7. Worland 22-24.

8. On the topic of ritualism, some critics have noted that horror films have a tendency to emphasize dates and anniversaries. (See: Falconer, Peter. "Fresh Meat: Dissecting the Horror Movie Virgin." *Virgin Territory: Representing Sexual Inexperience in Film*, edited by Tamar Jeffers McDonald, Wayne State University Press, 2010, pp. 132. Print.) We see some of that in *Hocus Pocus* (e.g. "It's been three hundred years, right down to the day").

9. Peter Falconer (Note 8, above) describes the Final Girl. She is smart, mechanically competent, practical, and sexually reluctant. She is marked as special and different from other girls. See: Falconer pp. 130-31.

10. Given that Winifred first attempts to sacrifice Dani before moving on to Max, it's probably fair to ask whether Dani is the "Final Girl." Falconer characterizes the Final Girl as "the Killer's most prized victim, the one he spends the longest time pursuing, the intended climax of his murderous spree." 132. Under that definition, we can certainly make a case for Dani as the Final Girl. Ultimately, we might argue the two share the role, which is certainly an appealing notion in light of the movie's theme of siblinghood (for more on that theme, see *Chapter Ten*). The fact that we can even have this discussion — that *Hocus Pocus* features a killer in pursuit of her prized victim while on a spree — evidences a relationship with the horror genre.

11. See: Holmes, Janet, and Miriam Meyerhoff, editors. *The Handbook of Language and Gender*. Blackwell Publishing Ltd, 2003, pp. 69, 173. Print.

12. The virginity theme speaks to Max's isolation too. After numerous jokes and jabs about his virginity throughout the movie, from a police officer and even his own little sister, Max finally shouts, "Look, I'll get it tattooed on my forehead, okay?" Like so many horror protagonists before him, Max's virginity separates him from his peers, and he is constantly reminded of it.

13. For Wood's theory, see: "The American Nightmare: Horror in the 70s." *Horror, The Film Reader*, edited by Mark Jancovich, Routledge, 2002, pp. 25-32. Print. For more on horror as a heavily codified genre, see: Falconer 123. For more on the "profound ambivalence" toward virginity in horror, see: Falconer 124.

14. As discussed in *Chapter Five*, Mrs. Dennison performs the "Vogue" dance in this scene. But notably, Madonna's iconic cone bras featured prominently in her controversial, Middle Eastern-styled performances of "Like a Virgin" during the early 1990s.

15. Cavell, Stanley. *Pursuits of Happiness: The Hollywood Comedy of Remarriage*. Harvard University Press, 1981 : pp. 116-117. Print. See also: Deleyto, Celestino. "The New Road

to Sexual Ecstacy: Virginity and Genre in *The 40 Year-Old Virgin.*" *Virgin Territory: Representing Sexual Inexperience in Film*, edited by Tamar Jeffers McDonald, Wayne State University Press, 2010, pp. 255-256. Print.

16. Phillips, Kendall R. *Projected Fears: Horror Films and American Culture*. Praeger Publishers, 2005 : pp. 1-3.

17. Also problematic in considering *Hocus Pocus* as horror: it's rated PG. Then again, so are *Poltergeist, Ghostbusters, Jaws, Beetlejuice, The Witches, Gremlins, Twilight Zone: The Movie, Something Wicked This Way Comes, Invasion of the Body Snatchers*, and *The Watcher in the Woods* — all movies that have been seriously treated as horror in one analysis or another. (In fairness, some of these were released before the MPAA created the PG-13 rating.) Certainly, many of the early Universal monster movies easily classify as PG, if not G. Steven Spielberg has described *Snow White and the Seven Dwarfs, Dumbo*, and *Bambi* (all rated G) as being among the most horrifying films of all time. For more, see: Wallace, Aaron. *The Thinking Fan's Guide to Walt Disney World: Magic Kingdom*. 2nd ed., The Intrepid Traveler, 2015 : pp. 139 – 140. Print. See also: Masters, Kim. "Steven Spielberg on DreamWorks' Past, Amblin's Present and His Own Future." *The Hollywood Reporter*, 15 June 2016. Web. 15 June 2016. <bit.ly/2bkYjuP>.

18. For a wonderful discussion of Disney as horror, see Davis, Amy M. *Good Girls & Wicked Witches: Women in Disney's Feature Animation*. John Libbey Publishing Ltd., 2006: pp. 22 – 27. Print.

Chapter 9 - Of All the Witches Working: Feminism in Disney's Villainesses

1. Davis, Amy M. *Good Girls & Wicked Witches: Women in Disney's Feature Animation*. John Libbey Publishing Ltd., 2006 : p. 1. Print.

2. Davis 108.

3. Davis 172.

4. Still, Ursula, inspired by a drag queen, is a revolutionary character in other respects. For more, see: *The Thinking Fan's Guide to Walt Disney World: Magic Kingdom*. 2nd ed., The Intrepid Traveler, 2015: pp. 127 – 132. Print.

5. The character of Esmerelda in *The Hunchback of Notre Dame* (1996), while not a witch, is accused of being one. On television, *Halloweentown* (1998) brought several new witches to The Disney Channel.

6. In discussing *Mermaid* and *Hocus Pocus* as back-to-back Disney witch texts, it is interest-

186 ※ HOCUS POCUS IN FOCUS

ing to observe that a woman's voice plays an important part in both. (Ariel loses hers to Ursula, while Sarah uses hers to cast a spell on Salem.) In literature, the voice sometimes symbolizes agency.

7. Davis 171.

8. Davis 231.

9. This notion garnered headlines in a recent controversy involving former Disney CEO Michael Eisner. In a conversation with actress Goldie Hawn at a public forum, Eisner said, "From my position, the hardest artist to find is a beautiful, funny woman." Eisner later contextualized those comments, explaining that he intended them only as a compliment to Hawn, not as a commentary on women in general. Still, the quip prompted substantial public outrage. (Eisner was CEO of the Walt Disney Company during the Midler years and at the time of *Hocus Pocus*'s release.)

10. The Bechdel test first appeared in a 1985 comic strip entitled *Dykes to Watch Out For*. The idea came to Bechdel after a conversation with her friend, Liz Wallace, and so it is sometimes called the Bechdel-Wallace test. They were inspired by the writings of Virginia Woolf. While the test is useful in analyzing the role women play in a given story and has been widely adopted in feminist film studies, it is important to realize a movie may pass the test and still contain other problematic or potentially sexist content. Critics of the test have proposed a number of variants to overcome its limitations. Bechdel maintains the point of the test is not to require every movie to check all its boxes. Rather, it is simply intended as a tool to help audiences think critically about the roles women play in movies and to become aware of gender-normative tendencies in mainstream cinema.

11. Davis 215.

12. The line is interesting from a Judeo-Christian perspective too. Indeed, *Hocus Pocus* is overflowing with religious references. An interesting aspect of the film is that, for all its focus on witchcraft and the devil, it ultimately upholds a Christian understanding of the afterlife and of the soul.

13. The "good witch" trope (also known as a "white which") emerged in part because of an evolution in cultural thought about witches, and about the Salem Witch Trials specifically. As people developed a more nuanced understanding of those historically accused of witchcraft, the idea of a "good witch" became more palatable.

14. One might read Mrs. Dennison as a feminist character too, at least in some respects. In contrast to what has been called the "86 the Mom Rule" in Disney films, she is the

more prominent of the two parents. And as previously noted, she is dressed as an icon of female empowerment. For more, see: Haas, Lynda. "Eighty-six the mother: Murder, matricide, and good mothers." *Academia.edu*, Web. 28 July 2016. <bit.ly/2aY8ya6>.

15. In children's entertainment, female villains and witches are often stepmothers, or otherwise a "bad" version of the mother (as in the Other Mother of 2009's *Coraline)*. The Sandersons do not have children, but it is Allison's mother who connects our protagonists to the witches. (Her mother ran the museum in the cottage.) We might read Winifred as a kind of "other mother" figure, then. For more, see: Davis 108-109.

16. Lest I offend friends and colleagues who wrote some of those reviews in 1993, let me clarify: I neither believe nor contend that dismissing *Hocus Pocus* as rubbish (or the pejorative of your choice) makes one (or one's review) sexist. The concern I address here is on a more global scale and is not localized to the individual film and/or critic.

Chapter 10 - Flora, Fauna, and Merryweather

1. Are they sisters? Yes, apparently! While never expressly clarified in *Sleeping Beauty* (1959), there is a family resemblance and sisterly vibe between them. The Walt Disney Company has since confirmed the trio as siblings, even including it in a storyline in the animated TV series, "House of Mouse."

2. It's not quite a mirror, mind you. Merryweather is *much* bolder than muttering Mary, for instance. The latter's passive aggressiveness now always reminds me of Stephen Root's classic character in *Office Space* ("I believe you have my stapler"). In fact, Merry might be more akin to Thislewit, Merryweather's counterpart in 2014's *Maleficent*.

3. Witchy Hecate Sisters turn up in many works of literature and fiction. In Gregory Maguire's *Wicked*, a maiden, mother, and crone attend Elphaba's birth. In the *Mary Poppins* novels, author P.L. Travers describes Poppins as a vain young woman, a wise mother, and a sharp-tongued old crone. The Fates in Disney's *Hercules* are of a similar model. The Weird Sisters, a fictional band in the *Harry Potter* universe, are a reference to the trope (and specifically to Shakespeare's characters in *Macbeth*). Some critics have observed that the Schuyler sisters in *Hamilton* reflect Hecate-like personas as well.

4. As long as we're making *Bedknobs and Broomsticks* comparisons, we might think of Max as passing through "The Age of Not Believing."

5. Scholar Chris Cuomo has suggested Eglantine Price is a coded lesbian whose lesbianism the narrative "cures" by the end of *Bedknobs and Broomsticks*. Certainly, there are historical connotations between spinsterhood and lesbianism; however, I do not find

any cinematic or narrative support for the idea that any of the sisters in *Sleeping Beauty* or *Hocus Pocus* are coded as lesbians (nor has Cuomo made that argument, to my knowledge). For more on Cuomo's reading of *Bedknobs*, see: Bell, Elizabeth, Lynda Haas, and Laura Sells, editors. *From Mouse to Mermaid: The Politics of Film, Gender, and Culture.* Indiana University Press, 1995 : pp. 217 – 222. Print.

Chapter 11 - Run Amok (Amok, Amok) in the Magic Kingdom: Walt Disney World's Villain Spelltacular

1. As this book goes to press, the Planet Hollywood at Walt Disney World is closed while it undergoes an extensive refurbishment and re-theming, part of the larger conversion of Downtown Disney to Disney Springs. Whether any of the *Hocus Pocus* memorabilia will return upon the restaurant's reopening remains to be seen.

2. The Not-So-Scary cover plays at the end of a fireworks show called HalloWishes, with a vocal that sounds quite a bit like Tina Turner (but isn't). The recording goes on to incorporate Maleficent and The Haunted Mansion's Madame Leota at the end. This convergence of Disney villainesses around the castle in "I Put a Spell on You" makes it a spiritual precursor to the Villain Spelltacular.

3. The gates look just like the ones in the movie, only they're missing the "Old Burial Hill" lettering across the top. I suppose that makes sense. Old Burial Hill is in Salem, and this is Magic Kingdom. Either way, it looks *great*. Halloween might be the only time of year when the Castle Forecourt Stage *doesn't* seem obstructive.

4. In the lead is Jennica McCleary, a professional Bette Midler impersonator who also performs under the stage name Divine Deception when not in Walt Disney World.

5. For more, see: *The Thinking Fan's Guide to Walt Disney World: Magic Kingdom.* 2nd ed., The Intrepid Traveler, 2015 : pp. 156 – 161, 213 - 222. Print.

6. Prior to Villain Spelltacular, the big stage show at Mickey's Not-So-Scary was The Disney Villains Mix and Mingle. It was a widely beloved show (and a little edgy in its own right). Disney fans don't often take kindly to popular attractions going away, but Villain Spelltacular really goes to show guests generally don't mind theme park attractions closing if they are replaced by something *truly* just as strong or even stronger. I don't believe I've encountered a single lament over the change.

7. In the show, the Sandersons' potion ingredients call for — and I quote — "nefarious nightmares, as terrifying as the shadows of the moon at night, filling dreams to the brim with fright." What a coincidence! Their recipe matches a Disney villain's anthem lyrics verbatim!

8. It's funny, too. Calling Oogie Boogie an "overstuffed potato sack" is classic Winifred.

9. Maleficent calls out a host of villains, who process to an adaptation of the movie's main title theme. The Sandersons call them "frightful friends": the Evil Queen, Hades, Cruella de Vil, Captain Hook, Jafar, and Lady Tremaine. Several of these characters appear as "furs" in theme park meet-and-greets (i.e., character performers wearing masks) but appear as "face characters" in this show instead (that is, the actors wear hair, makeup, and prosthetics, but no mask), underscoring the Villain Spelltacular's high standards of theatricality. Hades is especially noteworthy, as he is *not* presented as "The Master." In this way, the show acknowledges a distinction between Satan and Hades (the line sometimes gets muddled elsewhere).

10. "Season of the Witch" is a popular psychedelic rock song by Donovan, released in September 1966. Its appearance in Villain Spelltacular is in keeping with the movie's covers of existing Halloweeny songs (e.g. "I Put a Spell on You," "Witchcraft"). Of note: "Season of the Witch" also inspired a cover by Dr. John, an episode of "The Simpsons" entitled "Redneck and Broomsticks," and the subtitle for *Halloween III* (1982).

11. To my knowledge, Mark Willard was the first to observe that the dancer lighting the candle is the same one whose hair is plucked. @MWillardPhotos. "The dancer who lights all the candles onstage at the start of the show is also the "innocent" who Winifred takes a hair from. Hmmmm." *Twitter*, 25 Oct. 2015, 10:13 p.m. <bit.ly/2byUv9L>.

12. Thackery ends the show by telling the audience, with a chuckle, "Go forth and party 'til the witching hour tolls. Fare thee well, friends. Happy All Hallows' Eve!" (I think you're a little nonchalant about this whole Sanderson spell thing now that you're dead, T.B.!) This is a *very* effective way of integrating "I Put a Spell on You." It would have been so easy and perfectly credible for Winnie to simply sing it as a finale, but to weave it into the larger Not-So-Scary narrative so that she is purposely casting a spell on an unwilling audience is very germane.

Chapter 12 - But Who Lit the Pop-Culture Candle?

1. For a summary of popular critics' reviews of the film, see: "Hocus Pocus." *Rotten Tomatoes*, Web. 1 July 2016. <bit.ly/2bpqxWx>.

2. Hunter, Stephen. "Of whales and witches 'Hocus Pocus': Say magic words and hope it disappears." *The Baltimore Sun*, 16 July 1993. Web. 30 July 2016. <bit.ly/2blGo8c>.

3. Cult is also the root word in "culture" and "cultivate," both of which can help us understand the role of cult in "cult film" too. These are films audiences *cultivate* from

culture to define a culture of their own. For more on the etymological underpinnings, see Telotte, J.P. "Beyond All Reason: The Nature of the Cult." *The Cult Film Experience: Beyond All Reason*, edited by J.P. Telotte, University of Texas Press, 1991, p. 14. Print.

4.   Incidentally, Kenny Ortega is directing the 2016 live television production of *Rocky Horror Picture Show* on Fox (in pre-production as this book goes to press). Here again, the director gravitates toward a cult classic. For more on midnight movies and *Rocky Horror* as cult, see Telotte, above, generally.

5.   Then again, one *could* make an argument for it as a midnight movie. We do tend to watch it at the same time of year (even if not the same time of day or in a theater, and the story does contain some sexually subversive elements. But while it could be interesting to think of the movie in the midnight context, its legacy simply hasn't been a highly ritualized one.

6.   "A cultist accepts with… utter ease…. that the circuitous escape route described in the film's opening voice-over sufficiently accounts for Ilsa and Victor's arrival at Rick's Café Americain. Furthermore, a cultist will not feel uneasy to learn that Ilsa coincidentally received the news that her husband was alive and hiding in Paris on the very day she and Rick were to flee that city. Most certainly, a cultist can accept this and a good deal more…" Card, James. "Confessions of a *Casablanca* Cultist." *The Cult Film Experience: Beyond All Reason*, edited by J.P. Telotte. University of Texas Press, 1991: pp. 68 - 69. Print.

7.   Telotte 3.

8.   Camp enjoys a long history with LGBT audiences, and an occasional correlation with cult films as well. As previously noted, Kenny Ortega's works are noted for their camp value; many have become cult classics. Additionally, a gay audience might respond to the societal pressure Max feels to have sex (specifically, heterosexual sex).

9.   Other edgy Disney films include *Fantasia*, *The Three Caballeros*, *Something Wicked This Way Comes*, *The Devil and Max Devlin*, *The Making of Me*, *Miracle of the White Stallions*, *The Story of Menstruation*, *Bon Voyage!*, *Trenchcoat*, *The Watcher in the Woods*, *Never Cry Wolf*, *Dragonslayer*, *Tex*, and *One Magic Christmas*. For more, see: *The Thinking Fan's Guide to Walt Disney World: Magic Kingdom*. 2nd ed., The Intrepid Traveler, 2015 : pp. 133 – 142.

10.   When a reporter asked her to reflect on the movie's surge in popularity, Sarah Jessica Parker summed up the effect of the film's rule breaking on a cult audience: "Only since having joined Twitter fairly recently do I understand people's affection and devotion to

Hocus Pocus, and I can't really explain it, except perhaps it came out at a certain time…
maybe because it was sort of silly and odd and perverse and weird and we wanted to
eat small children, didn't we? Didn't we want the life and the air and the very breath
they breathe? Didn't we try to, like, suck it into our own bodies? I mean, that's freaking
weird." McCarthy, Kevin. "Sarah Jessica Parker interview – Hocus Pocus, Sex And The
City, SJP Collection." *YouTube*, uploaded by FOX 5 DC, 1 Sep. 2014. <bit.ly/2bz9xfF>.

11. Many movies call attention to their flaws as a way of embracing them. As James Card
(see Note 6 above) points out, *Casablanca* nods directly at its reliance on convenience
when Rick says, "Of all the gin joints in all the towns in all the world, she walks into
mine." By breaking the fourth wall, *Hocus Pocus* creates a less rigid atmosphere and
invites its audience to embrace its occasional anachronisms. Little asides like Winifred's
are a convention of film, anyway. It is understood that characters sometimes make jokes
for the audience's benefit, and inasmuch as those jokes are disregarded by the other
characters, we understand them as almost non-diegetic. Besides, it might even be narratively credible that Winifred knows about driver's permits. She's been out in the world
all night. She's encountered cars, been on a bus, and had conversations with modern
people. We don't follow the Sandersons at every moment; she might have learned.
We can make a similar argument in response to the frequent criticism that Winifred
shouldn't know Max used the phrase "just a bunch of hocus pocus" before lighting the
candle. Remember: by virtue of her spell, her soul has been alive within the hills of her
cottage (see the bonus section of *Fun Facts* in the back of this book for more). As good
cultists, we can easily thwart other common criticisms too (e.g. Cat Thackery doesn't
speak to his parents). But this reflexive kind of back-and-forth is silly. Films are sums
more than they are parts, and none of us love or hate a movie solely because of its plot
holes or continuity errors (or lack thereof). As Card says, "coincidence has served drama
ever since *Oedipus Rex*." Movies are artificial and nearly all of them goof or gaff at some
point. The more important question is whether they get away with it or not. Where
their audiences are concerned, at least, cult films do indeed "get away."

12. For a thoughtful discussion of that argument, see Telotte, above.

Epilogue: The Case for a Sequel

1. Clint. "Exclusive: Disney developing sequel to *Hocus Pocus*." *MovieHole.net*, 6 July 2012.
Web. 30 July 2016. <bit.ly/2aTtBJM>.

2. Satran, Joe. "'Hocus Pocus' Sequel Rumors Are Unfounded, Disney Says." *The Huffington Post*, 10 July 2012. Web. 30 July 2016. <huff.to/2bm5HG7>.

3. Barnes, Madison. "{TB Exclusive} 'Hocus Pocus' Sequel In Works After Years of Rumor." *The Tracking Board*, 2 April 2014. Web. 30 July 2016. <bit.ly/2bx5ej1>. See also: Whitehead, Donna. "{TB Exclusive} Tina Fey Will Bring a Little Magic to 'Hocus Pocus 2.'" *The Tracking Board*, 1 July 2014. Web. 30 July 2016. <bit.ly/1m9AX9n>.

4. Yamato, Jen. "Disney Developing Witch Pic With Tina Fey — But It's Not 'Hocus Pocus 2.'" *Deadline.com*, 2 July 2014. Web. 31 July 2016. <bit.ly/2b02CuF>.

5. Tough cookie parenting. "Um… am I the only one REALLY excited about this?" *Facebook*, 2 Aug. 2015. Web. 31 July 2016. <bit.ly/2bFeW6o>.

6. Midler, Bette. "It's the Girl! Bette Midler! AMA!" *Reddit*, 2015. Web. 31 July 2016. <bit.ly/2blQwhD>.

7. @BetteMidler. *Twitter*, 27 Oct. 2015, 6:51 p.m. <http://bit.ly/2aZjyOs>.

8. Midler, Bette. "It's LIVE Q&A TIME!…" *Facebook*, 17 Nov. 2015. Web. 31 July 2016. <bit.ly/2bx7WVw>.

9. Chaney, Jen. "The Magical Tale of How 'Hocus Pocus' Went From Box-Office Flop to Halloween Favorite." *Yahoo! Movies*, 28 Oct. 2015. Web. 31 July 2016. <yhoo.it/1ReihTh>.

10. Marcus, Bennett. "Sarah Jessica Parker: *Hocus Pocus 2* Is Just Internet Talk." *Vulture*, 28 Oct. 2015. Web. 31 July 2016. <http://bit.ly/2bcPRgO>.

11. LaCapria, Kim. "Witchful Thinking." *Snopes.com*, 4 Aug. 2015. Web. 31 July 2016. <bit.ly/2aYO5lG>.

12. Kelley, Seth. "Tina Fey Talks 'Kimmy Schmidt' Season 2 and 'Mean Girls' Musical at Tribeca Q&A." *Variety*, 19 April 2016. Web. 31 July 2016. <bit.ly/1pp0e4f>.

13. Domestically, *Sleepless in Seattle* was the top-grossing PG-rated movie of 1993. *Free Willy* came in at #2 (though with nearly $50 million less than *Sleepless*) and *Groundhog Day* at #3. Disney rounded out the Top Five with *Cool Runnings* (weirdly given the 10/1/93 release *Hocus Pocus* should have had) and *Sister Act 2: Back in the Habit*. Disney scored two more in the Top Ten: *The Three Musketeers* (#6) and *The Nightmare Before Christmas* (#10). *Hocus Pocus* was all the way down at #13 (and #39 for the year when all movie ratings are combined).

14. *My Boyfriend's Back, A Far Off Place, The Three Musketeers, The Adventures of Huck Finn, The Cemetery Club*, etc.

15. Winifred's last word before perishing is "boooOOOoook!" It is reasonable to infer,

then, that when the book opens its eye at the end credits, it is in answer to her call. The first time Winifred called to her book just before death (in the hanging scene), it summoned a spell to bring her back. Perhaps the implication at the end credits is that the book has done the same for her again?

16. *Into the Woods* is not the kind of franchise-oriented picture Disney tends to make these days, even if the subject matter is up their alley. The fact they made it is a surprise; the fact it became a big hit is an even greater surprise. As another Disney witch movie, perhaps it offers some modicum of encouragement. Perhaps if Meryl Streep co-starred in *Hocus Pocus 2*, the powers that be would deem the project worthwhile.

17. Rankin, Seija. "Enough With the Rumors Already-We Wrote the Plot for the *Hocus Pocus* Sequel." *E! News*, 30 Oct. 2015. Web. 30 July 2016. <eonli.ne/2bn5SCm>.

18. In fact, *Playbill* has tackled the topic twice! For more, see the Online Resources section in this book's *Bonus Materials*.

19. I don't intend this as a chide about age. Like all of us, the stars are twenty-some years older now than when the movie was made. Unquestionably, even now, makeup and prosthetics would be in order to return these wonderful women to their haggard 1693 counterparts.

20. Rob Reiner directed both *Sleepless in Seattle* and *Rumor Has It*.

Bonus Material

1. Press Kit. "About the Production." *Hocus Pocus*. Walt Disney Pictures, 1993. Print : pp. 10-11.

2. Greiving, Tim. Liner notes (print). *Hocus Pocus: Intrada Special Collection*. Intrada Records, 2013 : p. 4. CD

3. Greiving 4.

4. Chaney, Jen. "The Magical Tale of How 'Hocus Pocus' Went From Box-Office Flop to Halloween Favorite." *Yahoo! Movies*, 28 Oct. 2015. Web. 31 July 2016. <yhoo.it/1ReihTh>.

5. Greiving, Tim. *Hocus Pocus 20ᵗʰ Anniversary*. (Program). D23 and Creature Features, 2013. Print : p. 1.

6. Riley, Jenelle. "Leonardo DiCaprio Unleashes a Fearless 'Wolf' Performance." *Variety*, 11 Feb. 2014. Web. 31 July 2016. <bit.ly/MaiM54>.

7. Couric, Katie. "The Cast of Hocus Pocus on the Today Show (1993)." *YouTube*, uploaded by MrReto2812, 14 Oct. 2014. <bit.ly/2c8M6Zn>.

8. Mister D, "Kathy Najimy's Valentine to Bette Midler." *BootlegBetty*.com, 31 Aug. 2012. Web. 28 July 2016. <bit.ly/2chYOpZ>.

9. Fallon, Kevin. "'Hocus Pocus' Turns 20: Meet the Voice Behind Binx the Talking Cat." *The Daily Beast*, 31 Oct. 2013. Web. 28 July 2016. <thebea.st/2cyUjIe>.

10. Fallon, Note 9, above.

11. Fallon, Note 9 above.

12. Fallon, Note 9 above.

13. Press Kit 16.

14. Press Kit 16.

15. Couric, Note 7, above.

16. Press Kit 15.

17. Couric, Note 7, above.

18. Press Kit 13.

19. Press Kit 13-14.

20. Press Kit 12-13.

21. Cedeño, Kelvin, Albert Gutierrez, and Pedro Hernandez, "The Three CommentEARS Episode 10: Hocus Pocus." *The Three CommentEARS*, 22 Oct. 2014. Web. <bit.ly/2aSwWo9>.

22. See Note 21, above.

23. "Hocus Pocus 20th Anniversary– Complete Panel Discussion" *YouTube*, uploaded by MrHallow3, 24 Nov. 2014. <bit.ly/2bVBccL>.

24. Couric, Note 7, above.

25. Press Kit 20-21.

26. For one of these collector's reports, including scans of select pages from a shooting script, see: Petrie, Philip. "HOCUS POCUS — UNSEEN!" *PhilipPetrie*.com, 25 Sep. 2013. Web. <bit.ly/2ci5W5H>. See also: Halliwell, Paige. "Deleted Scenes." Web. <bit.ly/2c5knX4>. For additional deleted scenes details, see: Peitzman, Louis. "13 Behind-the-Scenes Secrets of 'Hocus Pocus' from Billy the Zombie." *BuzzFeed Entertainment*, 30 Oct. 2013. Web. <bzfd.it/2bRkghk>.

27. Boyar, Jay. 'Hocus Pocus' Gives Moviegoers a Bagful of Tricks and Treats." *Orlando Sentinel*, 16 July 1993. Web. 28 July 2016. <bit.ly/2cyYljV>.

28. Desta, Yohana. "Why You're Crazy Addicted to 'Hocus Pocus." *Mashable*, 22 Oct. 2014. Web. 27 July 2016. <on.mash.to/2cyZIME>.

29. Chaney, Note 4, above.

30. Chaney, Note 4, above.

31. Debney, John. Liner notes (print). *Hocus Pocus: Intrada Special Collection*. Intrada Records, 2013 : p. 16. CD.

32. Program, Note 6 above. 2.

33. Program, Note 6 above. 2.

34. "'Hocus Pocus Villain Spelltacular': The Inside Scoop." *D23*, Web. 20 July 2016. <bit.ly/1OoNDqC>.

Index

Acknowledgements

Writing a book is quite a process, and so many people make it possible, whether through aid or encouragement. I would first like to thank my editor, Sally E. Bahner, as well as Kelly Monaghan, Sally Scanlon, and everyone at both The Intrepid Traveler and Pensive Pen Publishing. My endless love and appreciation to my parents (Karen and Rodney), sister (Nichole), grandmother (Dolores), and late grandfather (Gary) for their countless *Hocus Pocus* viewings with me (among many other things). And my newer family members: my brother-in-law, Matt, and my two endlessly adorable nephews, Noah and Elijah (may they love *Hocus Pocus* someday too).

Having Thora Birch and Mick Garris on board for this project means the world to me. I would like to extend my thanks to both of them here, and also to Tina Williams and everyone at Rooted Films; Michael Adler and everyone at Berwick & Kovacik Inc.; Anna Dye and everyone at Echo Lake Entertainment; Mike Macaluso and everyone at Thruline Entertainment; and Vinessa Shaw. And Rob Yeo for his outstanding design work on the book's cover art.

I'd like to acknowledge the dear friends who helped with this book in a very direct, meaningful, and material way: Kyle Burbank, Christopher Disher, Albert Gutierrez, and Reuben Gutierrez.

Likewise, I couldn't possibly omit the "NJ Trilogy" (my Bette Midler movie marathon cohorts) or the larger Hollywood Tower Film Society.

I am fortunate to have such great educational resources available to me in carrying out research for these projects and the academic foundation they provided. Accordingly, I would like to acknowledge the University of North Carolina at Chapel Hill, Wake Forest University, and locally, the University of Central Florida — and, specifically, those who helped in various, indirect ways to prime me for this book many years ago: Daniel Wallace, Dr. Laurie Langbauer, Dr. Ken Hillis, and Dr. Sarah Sharma.

To all of my friends and colleagues in the worlds of publishing, Disney podcasting, travel and entertainment journalism, academia, law, fandom, and general geekery: my thanks both in retrospect and in advance for your support in this project.

And to the many other friends (and occasionally strangers) who listened to me rave and rattle on about *Hocus Pocus* for longer than could possibly have sustained their interest in any given conversation — I won't try to name you all here — thank you, thank you, thank you. Your encouragement means everything, and I am blessed to have you. And also to my friends who are no longer here, Mike Sullivan and Bryan Gandis.

To Kenny Ortega, Bette Midler, Kathy Najimy, Sarah Jessica Parker, Omri Katz, Jason Marsden, Larry Bagby, Tobias Jelinek, Sean Murray, Doug Jones, David Kirschner, Neil Cuthbert, John Debney, Marc Shaiman, Penny Marshall and her late brother, Bonnie Bruckheimer, and the entire cast and crew of *Hocus Pocus*: thank you for giving your fans so much to love and chew on. And to the cast members of Walt Disney World and Disney Imagineering: thank you for your hard work and talent in bringing the Villain Spelltacular to life. Naturally, this acknowledgment extends to Walt Disney himself, for leaving the legacy *Hocus Pocus* embraced.

To the fans and loyal listeners and readers who support my projects: thank you for allowing me the opportunity to dive into the things we all love. I hope to always find, share, and receive new perspectives with you all.

Finally and most importantly: my gratitude to the true Master, the God on whom I depend, and His Son, who loves us all.

CPSIA information can be obtained
at www.ICGtesting.com
Printed in the USA
BVOW03s2256230917
495731BV00001B/185/P